FINISHING WELL

*Aging and Reparation
in the Intergenerational Family*

FINISHING WELL

Aging and Reparation
in the Intergenerational Family

TERRY D. HARGRAVE, Ph.D.
WILLIAM T. ANDERSON, Ed.D.

BRUNNER/MAZEL, *Publishers* • NEW YORK

Library of Congress Cataloging-in-Publication Data

Hargrave, Terry D.
    Finishing well : aging and reparation in the intergenerational
family / Terry D. Hargrave, William T. Anderson
        p.   cm.
    Includes bibliographical references and indexes.
    ISBN 0-87630-683-0
    1. Family psychotherapy.   2. Aged—Family relationships.   3. Adult
children—Family relationships.   4. Intergenerational relations.
5. Contextual therapy.   I. Anderson, William T., Ed. D.   II. Title.
RC488.5.H355   1992
616.89'156—dc20   92-13976
                                                                CIP

Published by
BRUNNER/MAZEL, INC.
19 Union Square West
New York, New York 10003

Manufactured in the United States of America

10 9 8 7 6 5 4 3 2

To our wives, Sharon and Ruth,
and our intergenerational families.

CONTENTS

PREFACE

"All research and clinical beliefs come from the gut," our friend and colleague Glen Jennings is fond of saying. Certainly our work with aging families bears out his belief. We started our work armed with some foundational concepts about family therapy and older people and some experiences from our own intergenerational families. As our work in helping aging families progressed, our concepts, as well as our intergenerational families, were modified and changed.

My own transition into working with aging families started in 1984 when my grandfather on my mother's side was dying of stomach cancer. The doctors gave him the option of staying in the hospital or going home to die. He chose to go back to his home in the small town of Roy, New Mexico, where he had been a rancher for most of his life. My wife and I traveled with my mother to visit him for what I knew would be the last time. At the end of our visit, I was at a loss for words. I had problems in my relationship with my grandfather. I had never been fond of the way he treated me. I had always felt I was a disappointment to him. He failed to come to my wedding. I had never had an intimate moment with him and had never seen him have an intimate moment with anyone else. It was not that we fought or argued, but just that there was an unsettled issue that I could not quite put my finger on at the time.

I stepped up to his bedside and said, "Take care of yourself." After I stepped back, my mother took his hand and said, "Daddy, I will see you next week." She traveled to Roy each week so she had a reasonable expectation that she would see him again. My mother moved away from the bed. No tears were shed. Everything was neat—except for the unspoken.

Finally, my wife, who knows the pain of not being able to say goodbye to loved ones, went up to my grandfather's side with tears in her eyes. She took his chubby face into both of her hands and, tenderly staring into his eyes, said, "I love you, and I will miss you." The rest of us—my grandfather, my mother, and myself—stiffened. I have thought many times about my wife's statement and about our reactions. Most often, I have thought to myself that what my wife said is what I had wanted to say, "I love you and I will miss you."

What to most people is an obvious thing to express, I could not say. But I decided that I had to work on resolving that issue so that when it came time to say goodbye to my mother, I could indeed say those appropriate and meaningful words.

I quickly found out that saying goodbye to aging family members was not a problem that was limited to my family. In the process of working on my family issues, I found more and more family groups that were also struggling with the unresolved issues, stress and burnout, and new roles, as well as the losses and changes that come with aging. It was at this time that I was approached by a visionary developer who asked me to direct a personal-care facility he was building. The personal-care home offered the supervision and support of a nursing facility without the medical component, and it shared the property with regular family apartments and a complex that provided separate apartments and meals, but no supervision. The result was an older but still intergenerational community. I was given the responsibility of directing the facility and the opportunity to learn more about aging families and to help them in their adjustments as their oldest members approached the last of life.

The next three years were spent learning about older people and their families. After about one year, I started doing family therapy with intergenerational families. At this time, I asked my friend and colleague Bill Anderson to supervise the work and to explore with me the therapeutic techniques of working with older people. We eventually worked with 29 families over the next two years.

In some cases, we only worked with the older person, but in most we worked with the entire family in some capacity. The average number of sessions with individuals and families was nine. I worked with some individuals or families only one time, but I met with others for up to 33 sessions. The youngest older person I saw was 55; the eldest was 93. The youngest from the intergenerational family group that participated in therapy was eight years old. From the beginning of the project, we developed a therapeutic model integrating the philosophy and methodology from contextual therapy into a three-stage process of life validation, life review, and therapeutic intervention.

This book is the culmination of what we have learned about this therapeutic process. And although we do not view this as the only approach, it is hoped that it will help both the beginning and the experienced therapist conceptualize an effective method to begin working with an aging family. We have found the perspective outlined in this book to be beneficial and effective, but we recognize that much more work will have to be done to explore the systemic implications of aging intergenerational groups, therapeutic techniques with older people, and the impact of therapists' beliefs about older people in the midst of an aging society.

Part I deals with the therapeutic challenge of understanding families with aging members. Aging does not happen only to individuals, it also happens to families. Because of the changing demographics in the United States, four- and even five-generation families will become increasingly common. The first chapter looks at aging within the context of the family. The challenges that aging produces across the family life cycle are examined in this chapter, as are such salient intergenerational issues as death, emotional loss, and grandparenthood.

Ours is an aging society. Demographically speaking, every

therapist will be faced with helping families deal with issues related to aging. In Chapter 2 we try to summarize important information concerning older people in the United States. Demographic trends, the physical aspects of aging, and the psychological issues involved with aging are all reviewed so the therapist can understand the special needs of this population.

Chapter 3 presents the most basic elements of the therapeutic strategy we employed with older intergenerational families. Our strategy is rooted in the philosophy of contextual therapy and psychosocial development, but it includes the important techniques of life validation and life review. Although it is a difficult task to simplify contextual theory, we have attempted to do so in such a way as to explain the basic elements we used in our therapeutic philosophy and technique. The contextual approach is multidimensional, but the concept of relational ethics is especially applicable to intergenerational families.

Part II deals with the beginning stages of the therapeutic process. The basic stages of the therapeutic process—life validation, life review, and therapeutic intervention—are outlined in Chapter 4. Assessment of the aging family, therapeutic goals, and the role of the therapist through the three stages of therapy are discussed in this overview. Chapter 5 describes the first stage in our therapeutic technique, called *Life Validation* (Asnes, 1983). We use this technique not only to join with the older person, but also to develop the initial impressions concerning the dimension of relational ethics in the family. The chapter includes a brief discussion of major historical events that the therapist can use to initiate dialogue and access the rich long-term memories of older adults.

The well-known technique of *Life Review* (Butler, 1963) is considered in Chapter 6. Life review has been used as a standard therapeutic procedure with the elderly since the 1960s, but we use it in a contextual manner. This chapter describes how to utilize the life review process to spot intergenerational injustices or imbalances and to clarify possible points of therapeutic intervention. Also, the life-review process can be used with the intergenerational family to give multidirected partiality to all members' interests and issues. We do not describe this second stage of therapy as an intervention in and of itself, although the process of family reminiscence and subsequent crediting by the therapist can have a dramatic healing effect on the family.

The final stage of therapy in our framework is to intervene in the family. In Part III, several cases in which different therapeutic interventions were used are reviewed. In Chapter 7, *Multidirected Partiality*, the powerful contextual technique is applied with an elderly woman who was spitting on the floor in the personal-care home. Multidirected partiality is the key therapeutic technique in contextual therapy and it usually has dramatic effects in the emotional complex of the family.

In Chapter 8, the case of a widow who was placed in the personal-care home without her consent is examined. We view exoneration and forgiveness on the same path, although forgiveness is not entirely consistent with the contextual approach. We try to outline how a person proceeds on the road to healing family hurts that have broken relationships by moving through stages of insight, understanding, giving, and, finally, forgiveness. Although exoneration and forgiveness are powerful therapeutic tools, they are very difficult for the family and therapist to master.

Balancing obligations and entitlements is the subject of Chapter 9, in which the relationship between an elderly mother and her daughter is examined. It is difficult for the therapist to make an accurate assessment of the relational ethic dimension of a family, but many times imbalances are clearer. This chapter demonstrates how addressing these imbalances in a constructive way can be therapeutic for the family. Finally, in Chapter 10, we outline some possible future directions and implications for therapy with aging families.

No work such as this is ever accomplished without significant encouragement and assistance. We are indebted to Nancy Kriseman and Marilyn Bonjean for their review of certain chapters. Special thanks go to Ivan Boszormenyi-Nagy for his encouragement to apply the contextual framework to aging families and his suggestions on our "contextual-like" framework. We express special appreciation to Malcolm Street for his effort and vision in achieving community for an aging society. Finally, we acknowledge with heartfelt gratitude the contribution of the older people and their families who participated in our work. Their courage in facing the tough issues of aging and their ability to explore new vistas in family therapy make them true pioneers.

I entered the work of therapy with aging families to help older people finish well. Since that time, I have seen many families come down the stretch as the eldest member crossed the finishing line of life. I have found that I have been helped by their experiences and changed in ways that I hope will always remain with me.

TERRY D. HARGRAVE, PH.D.
August 1991

I

UNDERSTANDING AGING FAMILIES

1

THE INTERGENERATIONAL IMPACT OF AGING

Aging is not optional. Aging is like a vacuum; it eventually sucks all of us up. Despite medical advances and an ever-growing array of anti-aging lotions and potions, we all get old and we all die. This reality, no matter how hard we deny it, causes a tremendous amount of frustration. As we age, we lose physical and financial strength. We experience profound loss: job, role, status, friends, and spouse. Aging does not happen just to individuals, it happens to families right along with their elder members. The issues concerning relationships, the burden for care, and the stress of managing resources affect the family across the generations.

But even with the frustration and sense of loss that aging brings, the experience need not be entirely negative for the family. In the midst of the pain and the fear and the sadness, life gives the family one of the last great opportunities to resolve old issues and to empower one another with love and trust. The task of aging is not only for the family to survive the process, but to become stronger through the process.

MULTIGENERATIONAL FAMILIES

At family reunion picnics, often an intergenerational softball game is organized. Children, parents, grandparents, and maybe even great-grandparents play together. As each person comes to bat, most family members seem to root for each other. As the game proceeds, you usually observe an interesting phenomenon. The younger the family member at bat, the easier the pitcher tosses the ball. As each progressively older person comes to bat, the pitcher uses whatever finesse he or she can muster to try to strike the batter out. So young and old play at the same game, but the task of hitting the ball becomes more complex with age.

So it is with the intergenerational family ball game. Younger family members do not play in the minor leagues; they play right alongside the adults. Everyone aims for the same goals, but the tasks vary according to the age of the player. Developmental tasks for the younger children, while challenging to them, are easy for adults. The tasks become more complex and difficult with age. Just as in the game, adults and children take their "swings" at these tasks; sometimes they miss and sometimes they succeed. Members of stronger families stand beside one another, encouraging success. Weaker ones tend to blame players who are not up to par and give up easily. Young and old play at the same game. Each member has a turn at taking his or her "swings" at the appropriate times. The game gets tougher and more complex as the family ages. In our society, more and more extra innings are being added to the game.

"This is not only the century of old age, but the century of the multigenerational family" (Butler, 1985). As individuals age, families are carried along in the aging process. Aging touches every generation. In the therapeutic process with an older person, a therapist cannot afford to have a myopic, single-generation perspective. All families—but especially the aging family—present important issues of entitlement, care, security, trust, fairness, loyalty, and legacy across generational spans. Carter and McGoldrick (1988) reiterate this in their belief that the operative emotional field of the family at any given moment comprises the entire emotional system of three or more generations. When we talk about an aging family, we do not mean a family of a married older couple and one of their adult children. Aging families take in the entire multigenerational group. For therapists to understand aging and its presenting problems, they must consider the social, physical, and psychological impacts of each generation. In this chapter, we examine the normal family life cycle, the changes that aging forces in the family, the emotional bonds in the aging family, and the relationships between aging parents and adult children.

THE FAMILY LIFE CYCLE

Anderson and Hargrave (1990) describe how a hypothetical five-generation family of the 1990s might well look.

The 95-year-old great-great-grandmother has outlived her husband and many of her friends. She now faces the last stage of life and its ultimate challenge—letting go. Her 75-year-old widowed daughter is dealing with caring for her 95-year-old mother and her own need for independence. The daughter must deal with questions such as, "Where should I live?", "When do I have to give up my driver's license?", "Am I still an adult, even though my 50-year-old daughter has to provide some care for me?" The 50-year-old daughter, in turn, faces many challenges: helping her own adult children separate and establish themselves in occupations and homes, caring for her 75-year-old mother, working with her husband to prepare for retirement, and dealing with repressed sibling issues that tend to surface at this time. The 25-year-old son or daughter is looking for help to get started in life as they nurture small children, attempt to purchase a home, and wonder how they will be able to support the growing number of elderly. Finally, the young children of the fifth generation watch the intergenerational processes and absorb, albeit silently, the profound lessons being manifested across the five generations. (p. 311)

It is easy to see from this example that the multigenerational family deals with a multitude of concerns at any one time. Duvall and Hill (1948) were the first to propose eight stages of the family life cycle: (1) married couples; (2) families with small children; (3) families with preschool children; (4) families with school children; (5) families with adolescents; (6) families with young adult children; (7) middle-aged parents without children at home; and (8) aging family members. In a more systemic view, Carter and McGoldrick (1988) present the following developmental cycle of an intact middle-class American family, highlighting the processes and changes that must occur during the family's expansion, contraction, and realignment of relationships, in order to support each member's development in functional ways. As the authors of this developmental cycle point out, it is imperative that therapists recognize the extent of change and variation in the norms of the family life course, compared with the family of the 1950s. Some family patterns and themes are common, but therapeutic thinking about the "normal" contemporary family life cycle must include positive conceptual frames about some of the following issues: two-paycheck marriages; permanent single-parent households; unmarried couples and remarried couples; single-parent adoptions; and women of all ages living alone (Carter & McGoldrick, 1988).

Leaving Home: The Launching of the Single Young Adult

In this first stage of the family life cycle, the key emotional process is the transition of the young adult accepting emotional and financial responsibility for self. In order to implement this transition, several changes in the family system must occur.

First, there has to be differentiation of the young adult in relation to the family of origin. It is important to realize that this differentiation is a shift to an adult-to-adult status, rather than an emotional cutoff as described by Bowen (1978). Second, the young adult must develop intimate relationships with peers. Finally, for the launching to be successful, the young adult must establish financial independence—usually through securing work with adequate pay.

The Joining of Families Through Marriage: The Couple

The key emotional process in this second stage is the inclusion in and commitment to a new family system. In this framework, two family systems are joined by an overlapping third subsystem. Each system needs to negotiate and respect emerging boundaries for the new family in order to ensure its viability. As a result, the family changes during this stage must include realignment of relationships with family and friends; above all, the family needs to include the new spouse. Formation of a marital dyad with secure boundaries is essential.

Families with Young Children

The third stage of the family life cycle requires that adults move up one generation in order to become caretakers for the youngest generation. The family must modify itself so that it can accommodate new members. The couple must adjust the marital dyad to make space for children while maintaining the integrity of the marriage. The family must take responsibility for the children by managing a secure emotional, financial, and physical environment. Finally, the family must realign relationships to include the extended family in new parenting and grandparenting roles.

Families with Adolescents

When the family reaches this fourth stage, parents must shift the boundaries in the family to allow for more flexibility. Parents no longer can be the supreme authorities or caretakers in the adolescents' lives. Parents must now deal with the reality of their own parents' aging and need for care and dependence on the family. Adolescents move in and out of the system, seeking varying degrees of independence, whereas the oldest generation moves in and out of the system, seeking varying degrees of affirmation and care. In addition, the couple in the middle generation must refocus on the marital dyad and career issues, apart from child-care responsibilities that dominated earlier years.

Families at Midlife: Launching Children and Moving On

Carter and McGoldrick (1988) identify this fifth stage as not only the newest and longest stage in the family life cycle, but also as the most problematic. As the birth rate has decreased in the United States, the life span has increased, and so it is now common for parents to launch their children some 20 years before the parents' retirement. This requires the parents to find new life interests and activities. It may be the most problematic of all the stages because of the multiple exits from and entries into the family system. As children are launched, the couple must readjust the marital relationship to incorporate the evolving intimacy demands of being by themselves once again. The parents must now negotiate an adult-to-adult relationship with their children, shifting final authority, control, and responsibility to the offspring. As children move into new family relationships, the old family system must adapt to new relationships that now include in-laws and grandchildren.

Perhaps the newest and most difficult transition during this stage is dealing with aging parents. The family must adjust to dealing with the potential disabilities and inevitable death of the oldest generation. Responsibility for the care of the eldest family members most often falls on this middle, so-called sandwich generation (Dobson & Dobson, 1985).

The Family in Later Life

In this final stage, the family must accept the shifting generational roles and the shift of family power to the central and younger generations. As mentioned earlier, the individual member and the family must maintain optimal functioning in the face of physiological decline. This means providing care and nurturing for the older members without overfunctioning for them, and allowing them to make contributions to the family. The oldest generation must move into more of a support role for the middle generation; elder members need to be willing to serve the family by utilizing their own experience and wisdom. Finally, the family must prepare for the death of its eldest members. This includes life review and integration of real experiences with the past hopes and dreams.

THE IMPACT OF AGING ON THE LIFE CYCLE

It is easy to see how the aging process in the family multiplies the complexities of the family life cycle. Forty years ago, it was much less common for people to have living grandparents at the time when they started a family of procreation. With the increase in longevity, it is now rather common for a four-generation-family complex to exist. Along with the resources generated by the multigenerational family, the normative tasks and stresses put on each generation are made more difficult with each additional generation. The stresses that have an impact on the aging family include emotional issues, retirement, widowhood, grandparenthood, and changing roles.

Emotional Issues

Older people experience feelings similar to those of their children and grandchildren, but in ways that are appropriate to their years. One overriding theme that colors those feelings in old age is that of loss. The aging parent has lived long enough to experience most of life's losses: death of a spouse, other relatives, or friends; reduced social status; diminished physical health; and lowered standard of living. Perhaps the greatest challenge to the elderly person is coming to grips with his or her own approaching death.

Butler and Lewis (1991) note some common emotional reactions that older people experience in this last stage of life. Among the most common of these reactions are grief and mourning for the many losses that the older person has sustained. Grief is usually most pronounced when a spouse dies, though it also shows itself in response to losses of health, job income, or status. There is little societal or familial support for the aging person grieving the loss of a spouse in the United States today. In our youth-oriented culture, talk about death is avoided. So the older person is left to do much of this grief work alone.

However, all families and generations eventually experience grief and loss, and the lessons of letting go and mourning taught by the eldest generation can be profound. When the family and the individual approach death from a perspective of strength, they give past events of life appropriate meaning. Old unsettled issues, now talked about openly, can be resolved. Grieving and loss, though painful, become essentially empowering to the family group. On the other hand, if the family experiences the grief and loss of aging as overwhelming, discussion of mortality is skirted. The meaning of past events is left unarticulated; unfinished business remains just that—unfinished. Death then becomes an end that brings little emotional resolution for the family.

Guilt is another prominent feature in old age. As one draws near to the end of life, it is normal to feel guilt—for past failings, for the "sins" of a long life. Yet the older person may feel unable to make amends for these real or imagined hurts. As the elder seeks to consolidate the perspective of meaning and wisdom across the life span, he or she ideally maintains a realistic balance of human feelings. It is quite reasonable to expect that old age brings with it feelings and experiences of despair. The older person recalls things he or she wishes could have been different, considers present circumstances that cause pain, or ponders aspects of the future that are frightening (Erikson, Erikson, & Kivnick, 1986). However, these feelings of guilt, regret, and despair can be beneficial to the family if they are used as signals to address family wounds that have not been dealt with. The family will only lose hope if these issues are ignored.

Butler (1991) notes that in our individualistic society, loneliness (fear of isolation) can easily be a difficult emotion to handle. Americans have been conditioned to be self-sufficient through much of their childhood and adult life. Now in old age, the person often attempts to carry on in the same way. The reality of aging, however, can prove to be a severe blow to that sense of self, since aging people tend to become more dependent on others than they have been for many years. A very small percentage of older people require institutionalization, but over 86 percent experience chronic health problems; these often require health services and caregiving for daily needs by family members (Zarit & Zarit, 1982).

The emotionally charged state of dependence is a primary source of conflict for the aging family. In order for the dilemma to be resolved, the older person must accept the physical limitations of age and allow the family to give care when needed. In addition, family members must take appropriate responsibility for what they need to do for the older person and what the older person should continue to do for himself or herself (Walsh, 1988). The family avoids maximum stress when it maintains a healthy balance of dependency needs. For instance, if an older person doggedly struggles to maintain independence beyond his or her capability, the family is burdened with compensating for the elderly person's decline in mental or physical capacity. The following narrative of an adult daughter offers a glimpse of such a situation.

> Every time I would try to talk to mother about live-in help, she would cut me off. I would hire meal or cleaning services for her and she would terminate them the first time they came. I was reduced to dropping by my mother's home five to six times a day just to make sure she had not fallen or that she had remembered to turn off the stove burner or that she had not locked herself in the bathroom. My mother may have been independent, but I was her prisoner.

On the other hand, it is essential that the adult child or family not overfunction for the older person. If an older person becomes overly dependent, anxious children may become overly responsible. This can easily become a vicious circle: the more the family does for the older person, the more dependent the older person becomes. These family situations of overdependency, then, become breeding grounds for feelings of neediness, of being a burden, and of resentment (Walsh, 1988). Loss of independence often means loss of power or control. As older people face the limitations and perhaps indignities connected with advanced years, they may manifest feelings of anger or even rage.

Retirement

Retirement from work usually means a loss of meaningful job roles and relationships. The employment role can have special significance in terms of societal status and productivity. The retired husband and wife will be required to renegotiate the marital dyad issues and boundaries; in addition, the reduction in income will create additional family stress (Walsh, 1988).

During the preretirement years, an older couple most often will maintain separate spheres of influence and activity. Postretirement usually requires the couple to share the same sphere and, therefore, compete for the activity, influence, meaning, and satisfaction derived from the field. This postretirement field very often is the couple's home and the extended family (Walsh, 1988). If the couple is able to negotiate and share this field or redirect interests into new spheres of influence, the partners can negotiate this challenge successfully. However, if the couple cannot negotiate the marital dyad successfully in retirement, the likely result will be marital distress or overfocus on the younger generations of the family.

Retirement may bring other complex problems to the forefront. Although evidence suggests that the vast majority of people do not move after retirement, the significant portion who do go to warmer climates or retirement communities face the challenges of relating as a dislocated family, forming new friendships, and establishing different roles. In addition, the younger generations of the family may have to adjust to the retired generation, focusing on their activities and spending more time with grandchildren. This may give rise to additional time commitments and stresses for the younger generations. Since over 10 percent of all people over 65 have a surviving parent (Brody, 1985), the retired person may find that he or she has traded a satisfying work career for a demanding full-time caretaking role. This caretaking can also cause tremendous financial stress for a retired older person with limited resources.

Widowhood

Widowhood is a very different experience when one combines the variables of age and gender. As we have seen, loss is a major theme of an older person's life. When an older person combines the loss of a spouse with the multiple losses of home, role, status, and so forth, the dynamics of grief and the phases of resolution are very different. Older people may experience "bereavement overload" (Kastenbaum, 1977), wherein grief from one situation is mixed in with grief from another until none can be successfully processed (Myers, 1989).

Older women experience widowhood very differently from men. About 70 percent of women outlive their husbands (Treas & Bengston, 1987). Women are less likely to find a new marital partner, and they are more likely to have limited financial resources (Butler & Lewis, 1983).

Erikson, Erikson, and Kivnick (1986) identified two primary aspects of widowhood that surfaced in interviews conducted with older people. The first concerns adaptation to being alone after decades of being married. As an older person is able to move past the grief of losing a partner and reconnect with society, he or she demonstrates self-confidence and competence in dealing with intimacy and isolation issues. For those older people who experience the grief as overwhelming, isolation is the result; depression and permanent mourning become predominant life forces. Of those who adapt to being alone, most reorganize their lives and start "new" ones. They use the resources available to them at the time, making the best of their situation. For instance, a widow who may have cared for her ailing husband until he died may reorganize her life by caring for friends or people in need in her neighborhood. She fulfills a role in the community by effectively utilizing her resources and, at the same time, she defines a new and meaningful role for herself.

The other primary aspect of widowhood identified is the process of coming to terms with the feelings that surround the death of a spouse (Erikson, Erikson, & Kivnick, 1986). When people have been married for a long period of time, the death of a spouse may be experienced as "partial death" for the survivor. The following statement from a 93-year-old woman upon the death of her 95-year-old husband poignantly captures the survivor's feelings.

I never even considered the possibility that he could die. I never dreamed that there would be a time when we wouldn't be together. Now he's gone and there is only part of me left and I don't want to stay. What do I do?

The mourning process seems to evoke the reexperiencing of the feelings of sadness, guilt, passion, resentment, delight, fear, and other conflicting emotions that were a part of the years of marital love. For older people who had been married a long time, the reexperiencing that is part of mourning never seems to end; rather, a point is reached at which the feelings no longer dominate every aspect of life (Erikson, Erikson, & Kivnick, 1986).

Widowhood may mean profound changes for the family. First, aside from the grief associated with the passing of a member, widowhood may bring with it financial problems that affect the surviving spouse's life style and even cause the spouse to be dislocated from the home. Second, those spouses who have been cared for by the partner may not be able to function independently. Finally, the family may have to adjust to the older person's remarrying (Walsh, 1988). Remarriage often results in extreme shock for the family and family members may express a variety of emotional, physical, financial, and legal concerns. This adult daughter's statement clearly reflects the turmoil that she—and many in similar circumstances—feel when a widowed parent decides to remarry.

It's difficult to see my father remarry so soon after my mother died. Besides losing my mother, it's now like I have lost part of my father to another woman. What's going to happen to Mom's things? Am I going to inherit the estate or is my father's new wife? I want Dad happy, but it's really not fair.

Grandparenthood

Although data are somewhat unclear, it is reasonable to hypothesize that as much as 75 percent of the population over the age of 65 are grandparents (Troll, 1982). Because people become grandparents at different stages of life, the meaning of grandparenthood varies. For people who are midlife grandparents, the focus of extended family life may be on activity-oriented interactions; later-life grandparents may see grandchildren as opportunities to extend a legacy of care and nurturing to the family (Myers, 1989). Whereas grandparents can contribute to the care, guidance, and nurturing of grandchildren, they are not responsible for them. This responsibility rests with the parents (Erikson, Erikson, & Kivnick, 1986). Most grandparents see their grandchildren as an extension of themselves, offering a link to immortality (Timberlake, 1980).

Grandparenthood requires a range of boundary shifts in the intergenerational family system. Grandparents need to maintain connections through love and nurturing, without neutralizing parental responsibility and authority. Many parents become annoyed by grandparents' "advice" on child rearing. They may even become jealous when the older person attempts to be a good grandparent in ways in which they might have been lacking as a parent. In many cases, grandparents and grandchildren form such a strong coalition that the parental dyad is viewed by both with animosity (Walsh, 1988).

Because responsibility has not traditionally been a part of the role, grandparenting has been viewed as voluntary (Johnson, 1985). However, grandparenting is becoming increasingly more essential to the intergenerational family in contemporary society. As single-parent homes become more prevalent, the "outside" help of grandparents becomes more important. Many grandparents are pressed into the parent role as their children are unable or unwilling to care for the grandchildren. In addition, some adult children see grandparenting as an obligation they expect their parents to fulfill. These adult children can become quite angry when the grandparents do not become involved with the grandchildren.

When I was little, Grandma was always there for me. My parents are never there for me or my daughter. They're always off on a trip or they're busy at home. It's like they're not grandparents at all.

Changing Roles

As the parents age and the children mature, familial roles gradually change. Older parents claim that direct caretaking and parental influence diminish over the years. These same healthy and independent older adults express the desire that relationships with their adult children be characterized by open communication and noninterfering involvement. Most older adults start seeing their children as friends, rather than as subordinates (Blieszner & Mancini, 1987).

Most older people turn to their adult children for more involvement (Brubaker, 1985). Brody (1985) speaks of the sandwich generation of adult children, who feel the pressures of responsibility and care for both their aging parents and their own children. This pressure is especially strong on middle-aged adult daughters who "experience greater role conflict as a result of competing demands on their time. They tend to have primary responsibility for the emotional support of other family members, for household management, and for childrearing. In many cases, they are also full-time workers" (Barber, 1989, p. 251). Caring for the older generation represents a new normative stress for the middle generations (Brody, 1985).

Because of the inevitable physiological declines with aging, adult children often experience a role reversal with their adult parents. As the older people become less capable of caring for themselves, they become subordinate to and dependent on their children. Seltzer (1990) feels that the role-reversal concept has a negative implication; that older people experience a second childhood and should be treated like children. However, it is important to recognize that older people—no matter how frail—retain their adult status.

No matter how much care an older person needs, he or she does not become, and cannot become the child of the adult child in the feelings of either child or parent. Half a century or even more of a parent/child relationship cannot be erased or disregarded. People cannot become children to their children and children cannot become parents to their parents. Love for a parent is different from the love one experiences for one's child. (Brody, 1990, p. 17)

Older people may have many physical needs that are similar to those of young children; however, a needy, older person still retains emotional adulthood. In some cases, older people do need to give up power and control to others, but it is just as imperative that they be able to retain the respect and dignity of adulthood, even as they surrender some power and control. This is as true for the older person who has a simple hip fracture as it is for the older person who has profound Alzheimer's disease. Respect and dignity build trust into the intergenerational process of family, thus empowering future generations. Classic role reversal in which older people are treated like children robs the entire family of finishing life well. Family roles are more complex than a simple adult-parent to adult-child relationship. Family roles are always played out within an intergenerational context.

Caregiving for the frail elderly is an enormous task. Caregivers clearly risk experiencing more physical and emotional illness, premature aging, and a lower level of life satisfaction (Johnson, 1988). Most older people do not relish being dependent on caregivers (Myers, 1989). As a result, the aging family may experience high levels of strain when an older member requires care, thus fostering more interpersonal conflict and negative affect (Sheehan & Nuttall, 1988). Some of the issues that the caregiving family must confront are as follows: improving coping skills such as time management and relief from stress; dealing with family problems concerning the spouse, children, and siblings; responding to the older person's care needs (emotional, physical, and financial); facilitating the relationship with the older person; eliciting support; handling feelings of guilt and inadequacy; and planning for the future (Smith, Smith, & Toseland, 1991).

When families have a history of healthy and supportive relationships, the caregiving relationship may be more adaptive and less stressful (Myers, 1989). Caregivers can develop closer relationships with their parents, and perhaps their siblings, as a result of the aging experience (Horne, 1985).

EMOTIONAL BONDS IN THE AGING FAMILY

There is evidence that suggests that affection plays a central part for both generations in the parent–child relationship (Quinn, 1983). Other researchers have echoed this idea. Mancini and Blieszner (1989), Black and Bengston (1973), and Johnson and Bursk (1977) have all emphasized the importance of healthy emotional bonds between aging parents and their children.

Older adults are selective in how they give their attention to their adult children (Aldous, 1987). In this study of physically and financially healthy couples in their mid-60s, the parents seemed to give most of their attention to the adult children with the greatest needs, the single children, and those divorced with children. It is very often the case that these adult children in "greater need" are not the ones who become the eventual primary caretakers for the aging parent. Therefore, the caretaker may experience feelings of anger and resentment in response to the parent's showering care on and expressing concern for other, absent siblings. Sibling rivalries often surface at this time.

More research needs to be done about conflict and lack of affection between aging parents and their adult children. Some research reveals such themes as power struggles and patterns of blaming and disappointments centering on the failure to achieve (Hess & Waring, 1978). With an increasing number of aging parents and lack of boundaries in terms of authority and responsibility in the American kinship structure (Barber, 1989), it is easy to agree with the many researchers who believe that the future will bring increased strain in intergenerational relationships. Shanas (1979) observes that the family has become one of the few safe havens and private places for its adult members. The study of affection between aging parents and their adult children will become increasingly more important to those interested in promoting healthier intergenerational family relationships.

RELATIONSHIPS BETWEEN ADULT CHILDREN AND OLDER PARENTS

Older people, like many other special-needs groups and minorities, are easy targets for stereotyping. Myths abound about both the elderly and the aging family. Among mental health professionals, these myths lead to assumptions that aging families are poor investments for therapy, are resistant to change, or simply are untreatable (Walsh, 1988). Perhaps the most substantial mythology about aging families concerns the way that adult children and older parents associate and care for one another.

The first common myth is that the extended American family has degenerated; that intergenerational ties were once much stronger. This belief maintains that in preindustrial America, the family cared for its elders and respected their wisdom, much in the same way that some African tribal cultures revere their elder members. However, the truth is that America has never had multigenerational households in significant numbers (Treas, 1983). It has always had a nuclear family orientation; older people in the past did not generally live with chronic illness, as they do today.

A second myth concerns the frequency of contacts between older people and their adult children. This myth has it that because of the declining interest in the family and the geographic mobility of the family, nuclear families ignore and even abandon their elder members. In reporting on a study spanning three decades, Shanas (1980) notes that many older parents maintain close spatial proximity to their offspring. Eighteen percent of the elderly live with one of their children, 34 percent live within a ten minute drive from one of their children, and 75 percent had seen one of their children during the previous week.

Other studies support the notion that adult children, for the most part, do maintain regular contact and association with their aging parents. Cicirelli (1981) found that 70 percent of adult children surveyed in the Midwest visit their parents weekly. Troll, Miller, and Atchley (1979) note that 75 percent of older parents see their adult children on a weekly basis; if face-to-face contact is not possible, these parents use other means, such as letters or telephone calls, to stay in touch with their adult children. Mancini and Blieszner (1986) observe that local, regional, and national surveys of older parents all support the notion that contact between adult children and aging parents tends to be regular and frequent.

What is missing from this research is information on the quality of these contacts. Some research suggests that both the adult children and the aging parents have ambivalent feelings about such visits (Moss, Moss, & Moles, 1985). A desire to share at an intimate level is counterbalanced by a fear of being vulnerable or of not wanting to burden the other generation. Uncomfortable feelings and unresolved conflicts may persist long after a visit.

Several studies have looked for a connection between the frequency of contact and the well-being of the parents (Blau, 1981; Lee, 1979; Mancini, 1979). Dowd and LaRossa (1982) found that the frequency of intergenerational interaction was negatively related to the morale of the aging parents. However, Mancini and Blieszner (1989) hypothesize that frequency of contact between the adult children and aging parents may be more significantly related to the well-being of the intergenerational relationship, rather than to the well-being of the older parent exclusively.

The third common myth about aging families concerns the reciprocity in exchange patterns between adult children and aging parents. This belief maintains that older persons are an emotional strain on the family; they take more from the family than they give. Lee and Ellithorpe (1982) state that the level of "intergenerational exchange may bear directly upon the extent to which aging parents and their offspring truly care for one another and are willing to invest their own resources in furthering the well-being of the other"(p. 219). These authors claim that this parent–child exchange of resources may have different meanings for different family systems. If aging parents help their adult children, it may cause them to wonder if they taught their children sufficient independence. If the parents receive aid from the children, it could be indicative of either caring for the elderly parent or increased parental dependence on the adult child.

Most of the research indicates that older parents give more assistance to their adult children than they receive (Riley & Foner, 1968). Nevertheless, the exchange patterns work both ways, which is best characterized as mutual aid (Myers, 1988). In a study of *inter*family and *intra*family transfers of help, Morgan (1984) concluded that "we have not 'socialized' the responsibility for dependent members of society as far as we might think; families remain responsible for most of the burden"(p. 214). He notes that families who are financially well off tend to share some of their money with needy relatives, whereas poorer families tend to share their homes with needy relatives. Despite the increase in government programs for the elderly, most of the assistance still comes from family members. This aid exchanged between the generations probably contributes to the durability of family relations (Zopf, 1986). Butler & Lewis (1991) have stated that "the emerging picture of family life in the United States, as clarified by research, is one of separate households for all but the very old or sick, while at the same time maintaining a complex pattern of family relationships that are viable and supportive" (p. 35).

CONCLUSION

One cannot look at the problems of aging without seeing how they are connected with the intergenerational family. At every juncture and point of stress in aging, the family is connected in some way.

Therefore, to help the family, the therapist must relate aging to a life-span perspective. As Cicirelli (1981) suggested, the balance between child rearing and care for the older parents is necessary for the survival of the species and the fulfillment of the older person's life potential. The finely tuned sequential balance of giving and receiving in the intergenerational life span empowers individuals and helps to build a strong society.

Many have approached the intergenerational family as the source of emotional strength. When each generation's members act in a responsible manner, they show sensitivity to the needs and desires of one another (Thompson, 1989). Thompson (1989) points out that one of the problems in the American kinship structure is the great emphasis it puts on the marital bond and the youngest generation, which often leaves out the oldest generation: "We believe that families are the only source of emotional sustenance and intimacy and that older parents must stand far back in line for familial love and care" (p. 267).

In real families, what one is owed and what one is expected to contribute often become problematic and even conflictual. Communication can become a problem as family members may assume that they know the other person's interest; they may even deny or distort the needs of each other (Cicirelli, 1981). Empathy and open expression of needs and feelings in the aging family seem to be critical requirements in working toward a balance in intergenerational relationships.

The intergenerational family in the United States faces the challenges of extended aging in a time of great social stress. The next century will require that the entire intergenerational group join together to find resources to work through the enormous stresses of aging and other problems. Thompson (1989) clearly describes the challenge that faces the family:

The essential processes of intergenerational responsibility accrue as we move from attribution, through disclosure and empathy, to cooperation. Attribution is risky without disclosure. Empathy is impossible unless both partners engage in full and open disclosure. Cooperation flounders unless both partners comprehend the standpoint of the other. Finally, without cooperation, mutual responsibility cannot be realized. (p. 277)

2

OLDER PEOPLE COMING OF AGE

From our perspective in the last decade of this century, we cannot help but look forward to the 21st century and what it holds for the family. It seems that at no other time in history have so many issues and potential stressors complicated our lives, both as individuals and as members of families. Sparse economic resources; fewer societal and governmental supports; increasingly complex human relationships with extended, blended, and single-parent families; greater demands and stresses in the workplace; skyrocketing costs of health care—these are just a few of the overwhelming issues that face the modern family.

The dramatic increase in the number of older people in America is one of the profound changes that affects and shapes the economic, relational, emotional, and physical aspects of the family. There are more older people in the United States now than at any other time in history. As the population of older people grows, so too do the questions of how individuals and families will provide for members who live well into their 70s and for whom chronic illness, which adds to the individual and family economic burden, becomes a greater factor. Family units become more complex with the extended family reaching regularly into four and five generations. For the older people themselves, there are the demands of remaining vital and of maintaining caring familial relations long after the physical and mental vigor of middle age is gone.

However, in addition to potential stressors that come with an older population, there is tremendous potential. Older people can provide a source of family wisdom that empowers family members who thus learn about their past and the people and events that shaped their history. Moreover, they offer the family a source of love and nurturing as they lead the way along the emotional path of wrapping up life. And on a more practical level, they may relieve much of the family's stress by providing access to financial and physical resources through continued employment, or by contributing money, or taking on household responsibilities. In essence, then, older people offer a wealth of resources with which to meet the issues of the next century.

In order to help older people finish well, stereotypes and myths must be put aside. Older people are more like their younger counterparts than they are different. As is the case for the rest of the population, there are some older people who live life well and others who do not. Like all family members, they have a special role to play in the great drama called family. Some will play the role well, making their exits and entries right on cue. They will play opposite to the other family actors with great skill, enhancing the performances of the family as a whole, until it comes time to make the final exit. However, like any good performer, the presence of the actor will be felt until the concluding act; then it will linger on in the memories of others.

Some older people, on the other hand, will not play the role well. They will struggle with the cues. They will say lines wrong or at inappropriate times. When it is time for the exit, it will be unclear to the entire family how best to remove the actor. Should he or she be forced off the stage? Should the family take another "go" at the play? Should the exit be ignored? Like the good performance, the unsuccessful performance will linger on in the memories of those who watched.

Helping older people and aging families finish well demands that the therapist have a clear understanding of the people involved in the aging process. In this chapter, we examine the demographics of the aging society, as well as the physical and psychological aspects of aging.

THE DEMOGRAPHICS OF AGING

The population of the world is aging. However, there is more to the aging population than a simple increase in numbers. Among the basic factors that make up the demographic picture, in addition to the growth in the size of the aging population, are the change in the relative number of older persons, the increase in life expectancy, and the aging population redistribution (Longino, Soldo, & Manton, 1990).

Aging Population Growth and Relative Number Increases

The U. S. Bureau of the Census in 1900 reported that the total population of the country was 76 million persons, only 3 million of whom were 65 and older. These 3 million persons constituted only 4 percent of the total population, and were equally divided between men and women. By 1987, the Bureau was reporting that the total population was 243 million, of whom about 30 million were age 65 and older. Older people now make up 12 percent of the population, with females representing 60 percent of this group. By 2010 the projected population of older people over 65 is expected to represent about 14 percent of Americans.

This same demographic change is also occurring in the general world population. If all the older people in the world were gathered in one place, their number would make that place the fourth largest nation on earth, behind China, India, and the U.S.S.R.* The older population grew by 30 percent during the decade of the 1970s alone (Longino, Soldo, & Manton, 1990). By the mid-80s, there were over 290 million people over the age of 60. By the year

*As of 1991.

2020, demographic experts estimate that the world population will include over 600 million persons over the age of 65 (Kuhn, 1987).

But the number of older people over 65 is only part of the story. The age group of 85 and older is the fastest growing age category in the total population; it will remain that way well into the next century. By the year 2010, close to 7 million people will be over 85, representing almost 2.5 percent of the population (Special Committee on Aging, 1983). The number of centurions will likely increase from 37,000 in 1982 to a million by 2040 (U. S. Bureau of the Census, 1987a).

In 1900, the population structure of the United States was very youthful; in 1992, the rapid increase in the older population, combined with recent declines in fertility rates, has produced a clearly mature and aged population. In the mid-80s, one in every nine Americans was over 65. Assuming that the course of fertility continues relatively unchanged, by 2020 one in every five Americans will be over 65. Most of this increase will occur between 2010 and 2020, when the baby boom cohorts reach this category. The large number of births in the 1950s means that by 2040, one out of every five persons will be in the oldest age group (U. S. Bureau of the Census, 1987b). The graying of America is a clear and dramatic fact. When we consider that the group of elderly age 80 and over has the greatest need for hospital and care facility services, we see the tremendous challenge of providing for the older population's physical and financial difficulties.

Increases in Life Expectancy

The unprecedented gain in the life span is "nearly equal to the total number of years added to life expectancy during the preceding 5,000 years of human history, since the Bronze Age (3000 B.C. to 1900 A.D). We are truly in the midst of a longevity revolution" (Butler & Lewis, 1991). Improvements in the life expectancy for Americans, especially women, have been steady and substantial since 1950. In 1900, average life expectancy was a little more than

47. By 1985, the life expectancy for women was over 78, and for men it was over 71.

Although these life expectancy figures are impressive, even more sobering is the life expectancy of those people who live to age 65. In 1900, an average life expectancy for a 65-year-old was about 12 years. Now women who reach age 65 can expect to live an additional 18½ years; 65-year-old men will live about an average of 15 additional years (National Center for Health Statistics, 1988). This increase in life expectancy is creating a revolution in family relationships, as extended three-, four-, and even five- generation family constellations become more common, thus presenting families with intergenerational opportunities not possible before. These cross-generation relationships can deepen familial intimacy; they can also foster tension and conflict.

Longer life expectancy also places greater strain on civil support systems such as Social Security.

Older Population Redistribution

Although the states with the largest populations also have the highest number of older people (California, New York, Florida, Pennsylvania, and Texas), the ratio of older people to total state population does not necessarily correspond. Florida has the highest proportion of older people, followed by Pennsylvania, Rhode Island, Iowa, South Dakota, Missouri, and Nebraska. Most older adults live in metropolitan areas (Myers, 1989).

In making the transition to older adulthood from midlife, most people stay in their own homes. However, when people do move, it is usually for one of three reasons. The first is desirable physical surroundings, living amenities, or a friendship maintenance network. Most of the people who make these moves have intact marriages, are relatively healthy, and have adequate retirement incomes. The second reason behind making a move is physical deterioration to the point that the person needs assistance in carrying out everyday chores and functions. Most of these moves are due to health limitations; the person will relocate to a place where he or she can access informal care giving, usually from adult children. The third reason to move is that physical limitations are such that care or oversight of care by kin becomes essential (Longino, Soldo, & Manton, 1990).

PHYSICAL ASPECTS OF AGING

Physical aging is the process of change in the individual that lowers the probability of survival and the capacity for self-regulation, repair, and adaptation to environmental demands (Birren & Zarit, 1985). There are two primary theories on how aging progresses: One is that aging is genetically programmed at birth in the same way that puberty is; differences in longevity are due to the genetic inheritance from the parents. The other is that aging and the physical decline of the individual are due to the effects of disease on the human system. Although there is research supporting both sides, it is clear that the effects of aging on cellular structure make themselves felt in each system of the human body (Zarit & Zarit, 1987). Although older people certainly do not have all the same physical problems and do not age at the same rate, it is important to understand some of the major effects of aging on the human body in general.

Sensory Perception

Every sense—seeing, hearing, tasting, touching, and smelling—is vulnerable to the effects of aging. The decline in sensory sensitivity means that the older person must receive greater environmental stimulation to achieve the same impact that was made at lower sensory levels at a younger age. Faulty vision is one of the main problems of the aging. More than half of the cases of blindness in the United States develop after age 65 (Rockstein & Sussman, 1979). As aging progresses, the amount of light the eye takes in decreases and the sharpness of vision softens. Light/dark adaptations fall off significantly. Cataracts, detachment of the retina, and glaucoma are a few of the major problems that cause significant deterioration of eyesight in older people (Bigner, 1983).

About 50 percent of the elderly report hearing loss; the loss in men is more frequent and significant (U. S. Bureau of the Census, 1989). Common effects of hearing loss include the inability to hear high-frequency and low-intensity sounds. Hardening of the bones in the middle ear, as well as nerve damage in the inner ear, influences the degree of hearing loss (Newman & Newman, 1991). Taste and smell sensations also decline, primarily due to the decrease in density of taste buds in the mouth and in the number of nerve fibers in the nose (Newman & Newman, 1983).

Cardiovascular System

Collagen, a fibrous protein that is the basic component of connective tissue in the body, tends to lose its elasticity with age. Although changes in collagen affect the entire body, the cardiovascular system is especially vulnerable. As collagen surrounding the heart stiffens, fat is deposited on the heart's surface. There is a gradual increase in size in the aging heart; cardiac output decreases. This means decreased blood flow to the rest of the body and a reduction of oxygen levels in the blood. With changes in collagen, arterial walls also stiffen. Fat deposits are more likely to form in the arteries (Zarit & Zarit, 1987). Cardiovascular diseases are by far the leading causes of death among older people; however, the reduced flow of oxygen-rich blood to the brain, other vital organs, and extremities of the body contributes to a variety of health complications (Bigner, 1983).

Respiratory System

The change in collagen also has dynamic effects on the respiratory systems of older people. Lack of elasticity in the connective tissues contributes to a lower capacity for inhaling and exhaling. Muscle atrophy, weakened diaphragm, and poor posture contribute further to this lowered lung capacity. Reduced ability to inhale and exhale has a direct effect on the oxygen supply to the blood; this, in turn, has its effect on the rest of the body. Some of the more common respiratory disorders in older people are emphysema, bronchitis, and pneumonia (Zarit & Zarit, 1987).

Musculoskeletal System

Muscle atrophy and decreasing strength have long been considered part of the aging process. However, deVries (1983) has provided substantial research that indicates that if older adults remain active and continue vigorous exercise, they can retain muscle size and strength. This perspective suggests that muscle atrophy may be the result of decreasing physical activity among older people. Besides minor height changes due to spinal cord compression and poorer posture, most of the skeletal changes occur with the structure of the bone. The skeletal system of an older person tends to become more rigid and brittle. Loss of calcium in the bones leads to osteoporosis, which is particularly a problem for women, and this, in turn, contributes to additional risk of bone fractures. Scoliosis, back pain, and arthritis are the most common musculoskeletal complaints among the elderly (Bigner, 1983).

Genitourinary System

There seems to be a general decrease in the functioning of the genitourinary system that parallels age. The bladder and kidneys decrease in size (Rockstein & Sussman, 1979). There is a general lessening of blood flow through the kidneys, reducing their ability to filter and remove wastes from the blood. Urinary incontinence may surface in older people; men are especially prone to experiencing enlargement of the prostate gland, which reduces urine flow from the bladder (Bigner, 1983).

Nervous System

Because the brain is the vital center of almost every human endeavor, aging and its effect on the nervous system become very important. However, the performance of the brain in connection with learning, perception, memory, and language is perhaps the least understood part of the body. Most of the research on which current understanding of the brain depends is performed on animals (Willott, 1990). In addition, it is unclear whether deterioration in the nervous system is due to genetic factors, the environment, or disease.

Some conclusions can be tentatively drawn from the many findings through the years. First, it seems that as aging progresses, there is a decrease in the number of neurons in certain regions of the brain. These neurons, which are essential components of brain activity, are particularly prone to loss in the regions used for movement, perception, and language. Second, the "skeleton" of the neuron or neuronal cytoskeleton, so important to the storage and release of neurotransmitters, seems to be particularly vulnerable to the effects of aging. This skeleton is the mode of information transfer to the neurons. Third, the dendritic connections between neurons that allow them to transfer information to each other seem to decrease in number in some regions of the brain as aging occurs. Fourth, there is a possible reduction in the number of synapse sites in the aging brain. Synapses are the essential points of most neuronal communication (Willott, 1990). Finally, as aging progresses, there is a general decrease in the blood flow and oxygen to the brain.

Three of the major problems associated with the aging nervous system are Parkinson's disease, organic brain syndrome, and Alzheimer's disease. Parkinson's disease primarily affects motor activity; organic brain syndrome and Alzheimer's disease affect memory, orientation, emotional stability, and rational thinking. It is apparent that these problems have a profound effect an older people, but their causes and treatments remain elusive. For healthy older people, the changes in the nervous system are more benign. Reaction time and brain activity slow, but the process is not as dramatic as once thought. There is evidence to suggest that there is some decline in memory and fluid intelligence, however, these declines may not be profound. There is substantial research suggesting that older people can combat the effects of memory loss with continued mental activity and with the adoption of new memory strategies (Zarit & Zarit, 1987).

PSYCHOLOGICAL ASPECTS OF AGING

It is easy to see how a person's physical health affects the way he or she ages. For instance, we would expect an older person who is healthy and vigorous to have a greater degree of life satisfaction than someone who has health problems, such as heart disease or moderate dementia. However, as in the early and middle adult years, health is not the only factor that determines one's well-being. The focus of much of the literature on gerontology and aging has been on the psychological well-being of older people. Most of this work has tried to describe the correlates and determinants of why some older people are satisfied and well adjusted during the aging process, whereas others struggle with depression, dissatisfaction, and maladjustment. This section examines some of the major psychological aspects of aging.

Developmental Approaches

Several theorists have noted that, as one develops throughout the life span, one goes through different stages that arise in a somewhat uniform sequence. For instance, young children tend to develop language skills within approximately the same age range. Most developmental theorists have seen that each stage during the life span presents the individual with certain tasks or "developmental hurdles" that must be negotiated, if psychological well-being is to be achieved. If the "hurdles" are successfully "cleared," then the individual will develop appropriately and the chances of dealing with the next tasks in life will be greater. However, if the individual is unable to handle the pressures and strains at a certain stage, successful development will be curtailed and the likelihood of negotiating future life tasks will be in doubt. Several developmental approaches have focused on aging and later life.

Perhaps the most influential developmental theorist was a psychoanalytic student of Sigmund Freud, Erik Erikson. But Erikson (1963) differed from Freud in that he believed that the individual's drive to deal with environmental or social crisis is psychosexual urges, rather than the energy force behind development. Erikson envisioned that at each life stage, the individual is presented with psychosocial crisis. If a person could deal successfully with the crisis the environment presented, then development continues. However, Erikson maintained that each psychosocial crisis at each stage had to be addressed and resolved in order to deal with the next life stage.

Erikson conceptualized the life experience as having eight separate stages: trust versus mistrust (infancy), autonomy versus shame or doubt (toddlerhood), initiative versus guilt (preschool childhood), industry versus inferiority (school age childhood), identity versus role confusion (adolescence), intimacy versus isolation (young adulthood), generativity versus stagnation (middle adulthood), and ego integrity versus despair (later adulthood).

The last stage, *integrity versus despair,* is the fulfillment and culmination of the preceding seven stages. Ego integrity is achieved when an individual makes identification with humankind and has come to grips with the contribution he or she has made to society. During this stage the individual is forced to arrive at some type of reconciliation with the realities of actual life, in comparison with what he or she had hoped to accomplish. The individual evaluates his or her identity and performance over the life span. If an older person is able to resolve this difficult crisis, a sense of peace and integrity about identity is achieved. If the person is unable to reach this point of reconciliation, then a sense of loss, disappointment, and dissatisfaction will result, and the person is reduced to living his or her life in despair. The rest of life is spent recalling the regret and fear of the life span, and feeling that change is hopeless.

Although Erikson's framework for the last stage of life is helpful, he provided little specific information about the resolution of this stage. Peck (1968) extended the life stage of old age into three psychological conflicts. Peck believed that the older person needs to negotiate these three themes if he or she is to reach the last stage with a sense of integrity. The first task Peck identified was *ego differentiation versus work role preoccupation*. For most, aging means an ebbing of one's ability to perform work and tasks at the same level that they were performed in younger years. Successful aging means that the older person is able to redefine his or her sense of personal worth, shifting the focus from what he or she "does"to what he or she "is" as an individual.

Peck's second task is *body transcendence versus body preoccupation*. As we have already seen, the body deteriorates as the aging process proceeds. In order to be satisfied during the aging process, an older person must redefine happiness apart from the context of good health. For instance, a person may not be able to walk any longer because of physical limitations; however, he or she may take joy in the ability to keep a good sense of humor and make others laugh. The older person needs to concentrate on the human capacities that remain in old age, rather than focus on physical capabilities that may have been diminished or lost.

The final theme is *ego transcendence versus ego preoccupation*. Death is inevitable. As death nears for the older person, he or she will either adapt to the realization that life will go on through others, or become rigid in denial of death and try to hang onto life through inappropriate or dysfunctional means. If the person can transcend ego, then he or she will realize the worth of family and likely will focus on passing down elements of wisdom to younger generations.

Influenced by Erik Erikson's theory, Robert Butler (1963) noted that older people go through a universal process of life reminiscence or *life review*. This process is brought on by the knowledge of approaching death. It is the individual's effort to reconcile the idealized self with the actual contribution to life. This life review is particularly difficult around unresolved issues in the past. Life review has been one of the primary therapeutic tools used in therapy with older people. We examine it in depth in Chapter 6.

Robert Havighurst (1972) was one of the first developmental theorists to describe growth throughout the entire life span. He believed that the interaction between the environment and the individual causes growth. As the individual develops physically, cognitively, and emotionally, the environment or society presents the person with age-appropriate tasks. These have to be negotiated successfully if the person is to mature and develop. Although failure to negotiate a task would not prevent a person from developing in the next stage, it would impede the person's performance in future tasks. Havighurst outlined six stages of development. The tasks that deal with the last stage of older adulthood are as follows: (1) adjust to declining strength and health; (2) adjust to reduced income; (3) adjust to the death of a spouse and the resulting grief; (4) establish an explicit affiliation with one's own age group; (5) establish satisfactory and acceptable living arrangements; and (6) maintain and meet continuing social and family obligations.

Personality Approaches

Personality refers to the distinctive characteristics and patterns of behavior that an individual adopts in reference to life situations (Mischel, 1981). Very little is known about the dimensions, variations, and dynamics that contribute to personality traits. However, it is helpful to use the information we do have to try to develop parameters of personality or personality types. When we consider personality during old age, it is also important to note that there is substantial evidence indicating that one's personality is stable over the life span (France, 1990). Even so, there are some helpful classifications of personality types that may further understanding of older people.

Probably the most commonly used typology for the personality of older people was developed by Neugarten, Havighurst, and Tobin (1968). These researchers concluded that personality type was the crucial factor in successful aging. They referred to four major personality types, with eight different subcategories or lifestyle patterns.

The first major personality type is the *integrated* personality. People with integrated personalities are generally able to accept their strengths and weaknesses. They maintain intimate relationships with family and others, remaining well adjusted as they grow older. Most of these people experience high degrees of life satisfaction. There are three subcategories of integrated personalities. *Reorganizers* are competent, engaged, and involved. They substitute new, relevant activities for the activities they no longer can perform. *Focused* integrated people are only moderately active, either by choice or because of physical limitations. They spend their time centered on only one or two life roles. *Disengaged* people have a significantly low level of activity and role involvement. However, they also have high self-esteem and are satisfied to withdraw from role commitment in old age because they believe it is a part of the natural process of aging.

The second major personality type is the *armored-defended* personality. Generally, people in this category see aging as an enemy with which they fight. They struggle to maintain activities that reflect middle-age roles, trying to stave off the aging process by using an array of defense mechanisms. There are two subcategories of armored-defended personalities. *Holding on* describes older people who struggle to maintain their mid-life activities. When they are successful in maintaining these roles, they have adequate levels of life satisfaction. Depression and anger are usual coping mechanisms when these people cannot maintain the roles they wish. *Constricted* people are those who become preoccupied with the losses and deficits brought on by aging. They most often complain about what they cannot do, longing for the days when they were able to perform "useful" roles.

Passive-dependent is the third major category of personality type. Older people with this personality have little commitment to taking care of themselves cognitively, emotionally, socially, or physically. They are usually highly dependent on caregivers and their families. They have medium to low levels of life satisfaction. One of the subcategories of this personality type is *succor-seeking*. These older people maintain a high activity level as they seek to gain the attention of caregivers or family. They may use a variety of manipulative techniques to gain attention. *Apathetic* people maintain low role activity, displaying little interest in life in general. While this subcategory places little expectation on their families, their lack of care for themselves requires that caregivers be more active.

The final personality type is the *unintegrated* personality. Those in this category have usually lost the ability to contribute to a role. Sickness and disease are prevalent among this group; life satisfaction is very low. The one subcategory of this type is the *disorganized* personality. Disorganized older people have deteriorated cognitive and physical processes, with poor emotional control.

Close parallels of personality types were found by Reichard, Livson, and Peterson (1962) in their study of older men. They proposed five personality types. *Mature* personalities are those who adjust well to aging. *Rocking-chair* types are more passive than mature types, but are satisfied to be more disengaged as aging occurs. *Armored* types are highly self-controlled, seeking to maintain middle-age activities. *Angry* personality types, frustrated with the aging process, tend to lash out and blame others. Finally, *self-hater* types are poorly adjusted to aging, tending to focus blame inward.

Major Psychological Issues for Older People

Psychological problems are not restricted to late adulthood. However, there are salient physical and developmental issues that tend to be predominant as adults grow older. Schefft and Lehr (1990) present some of the major psychological problems experienced by the elderly.

Loss and depression.

Loss becomes one of the central themes as older people experience the myriad changes that accompany age. Loss of job or family status, of independence, of physical strength, of health, and of loved ones are among the changes that might be anticipated. It is not surprising, then, that depression is the most common psychiatric complaint of older people. Estimates of depression among older people set the prevalence at about twice that for the general population. At least 25 percent of the suicides in the United States are committed by people over 65. Males over age 75 are most at risk.

Control difficulties.

As people age, there are many potential threats to independence. Illness and retirement, for example, may limit a person's ability to control his or her physical and financial circumstances. There is also evidence suggesting that as people age, they may use fewer coping strategies in managing stressors. With fewer coping skills comes less control over the environment. Since maintaining a sense of personal control is one of the primary factors in life satisfaction among the elderly (Thomae, 1985), lack of control contributes significantly to psychological stress.

Chronic illness.

Physical health has many impacts on the human condition. Where we live and work and the roles we maintain are somewhat dependent on our health. Besides the pain and discomfort, chronic illness may contribute to an older person's feeling of a reduced sense of control and less mastery in the environment. Chronic illness in the older person can be a signal that death is imminent. Finally, an older person may fear the unknown or feel guilty about being a burden on the family or caregivers.

Organic behavioral and emotional problems.

Organic brain disorders such as dementia, stroke, or Alzheimer's can cause dramatic behavioral problems. Confusion and disorientation leading to an overall disorganization of behavior may result in fear, withdrawal, or outbursts of anger designed to strike out at others. Impulsiveness and poor behavioral or emotional control may be symptoms of these organic disorders.

CONCLUSION

Caring for an aging population is just one of the many challenges that confronts modern society, but the magnitude of the issues that accompany such care is great. Just the sheer size of the aging population necessitates that the economic and familial patterns adapt quickly. It is essential that the therapist understand these profound societal changes. In addition, the therapist needs to be sensitive to individual and family stresses produced by the physical and psychological impacts of aging. Growing old in the 1990s and beyond will be very different than in the past. The psychological community must be prepared to empower aging individuals and families to meet these challenges.

3

THE THEORETICAL
FRAMEWORK

The task of bringing about change in any family seeking therapy is substantial. But when an aging family comes to therapy, the process of change becomes enormously more complex. Besides being faced with presenting problems of the older person, symptomatic behavior of the family, personality conflicts, and dysfunctional transactions, the therapist and aging family must also deal with the variety of developmental concerns spanning three, four, and perhaps five generations. Family-of-origin issues, which may only surface slightly in a two-generation family, can become dominant themes as the intergenerational aging family plays out these conflicts in front of the therapist. Death, grief, reflection, despair, frustration, anxiety, physical deterioration, years of unresolved family conflict—all are present in force with an aging family in therapy. In short, aging families present the therapist with a much more complex system than do other families. It is not only that the problems of aging might be tougher, but the changes that the family needs to implement must be more far-reaching, affecting several more dimensions of the system.

Although the aging family presents a more complicated set of problems and concerns, it also offers a unique opportunity to the therapist in that it contains more relationships and, therefore, more points of therapeutic entry. The presence of a significant number of the members of the intergenerational family means that there exists a great deal of therapeutic power to change relationships significantly, and with the presence of the intergenerational family unit, the therapist has available the resources to empower the unit itself to access family strength. The therapist can also build trustworthy relations in place of the dysfunctional and despairing interactions that are so often passed from one generation to the next. The goal of this chapter is to offer the basic theoretical background of contextual family therapy, in order to help therapists understand the problems and mobilize the family for positive outcomes.

INTERGENERATIONAL FAMILY THERAPY THEORY

As therapists, we are all interested in techniques that work in family therapy. But in our quest for better techniques, we sometimes ignore the theory and philosophy behind different therapies. In doing so, many therapists have become "technique junkies," always looking for the next technique. It seems to us that this type of therapy is like learning only one chord or one note on a musical instrument. Although knowing one note or chord allows a person to make a sound, it does not facilitate an understanding of the intricacies involved in mastering an instrument. In order to play, musicians must understand the dynamics of the instrument and how its unique character fits into the larger scheme of music.

We view family therapy theory in this manner. It is not that we believe theory is so great in and of itself; rather, theory allows the therapist to organize his or her talents in such a way that will fit in with, make sense of, and help change the family. Just as an orchestra has different instruments, the family therapy field has different theories. Some theories are more popular than others, but most have a unique place in the field. It is our view that it is necessary and essential for the therapist to organize a therapeutic framework that gives proper consideration to the complex dimensions of an aging family. Because of the heavy intergenerational dynamics involved with aging families, we feel the most comfortable with the intergenerational theories. However, we are quick to point out that the approach developed in this book is only one among many therapeutic approaches.

There are several intergenerational theories that have made unique impacts on the field, perhaps the best known of which is Bowen's family systems theory. Murray Bowen (1978) believed that as individuals resolve undifferentiated relationships with their families of origin, they become more differentiated, flexible, able to cope with stress, and have fewer personal and marital problems. His work focused on the emotional forces that influence both nuclear and intergenerational families. Several therapists have proposed using Bowen's framework in therapy with aging families; most notable among these are Long and Mancini (1990).

James Framo's (1981) contribution to intergenerational theory is highly significant. His work focuses on the development of intrapsychic conflicts in individuals in their families of origin that are later played or acted out in other relationships. He uses many of the tenets of object relations theory, combined with the technique of group family-of-origin sessions in his therapy. Most of this intergenerational family work has been applied to the marital therapy context (Framo, 1976). More recently, Donald Williamson (1981) has made significant contributions to intergenerational theory by examining the concept of personal authority in the family of origin. Williamson sees successful differentiation and adjustment as dependent on an individual's ability to take an adult position with his or her parents. These last two approaches, although important to the understanding of intergenerational relations, have not been specifically applied to aging families.

The intergenerational approach known as contextual family therapy was developed primarily by Ivan Boszormenyi-Nagy. As one of the founders of the family therapy movement in the United States, Boszormenyi-Nagy developed his therapeutic style from psychiatry, psychoanalysis, systems theory, and philosophy (Boszormenyi-Nagy & Krasner, 1986). His personal evolution as a therapist led him to develop an integrative approach in dealing with the complexity of human existence between individual and relational realities. The essence of the contextual approach is to heal human relationships by mobilizing family resources such as commitment and trust, while building interpersonal components of loyalty, fairness, and reciprocity (Boszormenyi-Nagy & Spark, 1984). Contextual therapy was not developed as a theory as such (Ulrich, 1983), but it has clearly evolved into a major theoretical and therapeutic approach (Kaslow, 1987).

Contextual therapy often has been criticized as being too intellectual and too confusing—partly because of its use of a different therapeutic language. The contextual approach has also been viewed by some as a "theory of theories" or a compilation of different approaches (Gurman & Kniskern, 1981). But the concepts of trust, fairness, loyalty, and reciprocity are universally powerful and especially applicable to the aging family. The contextual framework gives the therapist a unique insight into helping an aging family balance unfinished business, heal and forgive old wounds, and finish life well. Some new language and ideas are essential to understanding the basic structure of the contextual approach, but the theory is not as confusing as it first may appear.

THE CONTEXTUAL THERAPY THEORY OF RELATIONSHIPS

Contextual therapy is a comprehensive family therapy approach that integrates several significant premises from different theories of psychotherapy. The foundational premise of the contextual approach is that there are four dimensions of relational reality that must be considered in therapy: facts, individual psychology, family or systemic transactions, and relational ethics (Boszormenyi-Nagy & Ulrich, 1981). Although these four dimensions are discussed separately, they are intertwined and inseparable in terms of their effect on the family. In other words, the dimensions affect the entire emotional field of the family; the whole of the dimensions is greater that the sum of the different parts.

Facts

This first dimension of relationships is anchored in existing environmental, relational, and individual factors that are objectifiable. They include such factors as genetic input, physical health, basic historical facts, and events in a person's life cycle (Boszormenyi-Nagy & Krasner, 1986).

Aging families have a multitude of factors that affect the relationships. What is the medical history of the older person? Is the cognitive structure of the older person intact? Does the older person have adequate financial resources? Does the family live close by or some distance away? Is the older person widowed? These and many more questions spring to mind when talking about the facts that affect family relationships. Facts are primarily a matter of destiny. In other words, family members usually do not have control over such factors as racial heritage, socioeconomic classification, and health. Some older people, and thus their families, suffer blindness, organic brain deterioration, or chronic illness that demand constant family attention, whereas others experience long periods of health with no medical or family care being needed.

It has been our observation that in many aging families, factual concerns tend to dominate the relationships. It is easy to understand why this is true. Impaired health and the medical attention it requires forces enormous time commitments in doctors' appointments alone. It is not unusual for an older person who has a chronic health problem to receive care from several different physicians. As most physicians prescribe medication for health problems, attention must be given to taking the medications in the proper doses at the proper times. Eight out of every ten people over the age of 65 are on at least three daily medications (Petersen, 1987).

Then there are the concerns that families have over the older adult's living situation. Is the older person safe from crime? Is the person capable of living on his or her own? Should the person move and, if so, where? When independent living becomes an issue, it is not unusual for these questions to dominate the family relationships for months or even years. And in addition to the specific questions about the medical and living conditions, the costs associated with each area must be taken into account. If an older person does not have adequate financial resources, the intergenerational family may experience substantial stress as it seeks to provide adequate care.

It is quite understandable that aging families sometimes have difficulty in meeting some of the obligations and coping with the stresses that life brings them. The most basic functioning may require all of the energy the family has. There may be little time left for consideration of the psychological or emotional issues that must be dealt with between members, issues that include needs such as intimacy, warmth, and love.

Individual Psychology

This dimension represents the subjective internal psychological integration of experiences and motivations of individuals in the family. The individual psychology of each family member produces subjective influences on relationships. Individuals strive for recognition, love, power, and pleasure and are motivated by aggression, mastery, or ambivalence (Boszormenyi-Nagy & Krasner, 1986).

The contextual approach in this dimension has been heavily influenced by psychoanalytic thought. Fairbairn's (1963) approach to object relations is especially noteworthy for the contextual therapist. Although several psychoanalytic influences are present in this dimension, the one most applicable and appropriate with the aging family seems to be Erikson's (1963) psychosocial development. A short overview of the stages is included here to remind the therapist that each generation is dealing with different pertinent issues and individual concerns. In order for a therapist to give proper recognition to each generation, he or she must be sensitive to the psychological struggle of each person.

Erik Erikson (1963) suggested that development is an evolutionary process based on universally experienced sequences of biological, social, and psychological events that take place between birth and death. This *epigenetic principle* suggests that development is a function of progression through time of a differentiation of parts (Erikson, 1985). Each part of individual development is systematically related to all other parts so that whole is dependent on the proper development in the proper sequence of each item. Erikson believes that the sequence of development occurs in eight major stages of psychosocial crisis. Each psychosocial crisis presents the developing individual with a central task that, if negotiated, gives rise to competence, identity, and strength, enhancing the prospects of future development. However, if the psychosocial crisis is overwhelming and the central task is not negotiated by the individual, the person will experience retarded growth and subsequent difficulty in dealing with future crises.

Psychosocial development suggests that individuals progress through each crisis within the context of the environmental reality and the people who share that reality (Erikson, 1985). Therefore, the individual, others, and reality combine in a mutually activating and stimulating process that produces individual personalities and shapes the environment in which the individual lives.

The first stage of development that occurs during infancy presents the individual with the psychosocial crisis of *trust versus mistrust*. Simply stated, if the infant receives consistent care and love and has sufficient opportunity to respond to the care in a contented manner, trust is consolidated into the personality. If, however, the infant does not receive the care and warmth deserved, then mistrust of the environment results. Infants develop a sense of hope when basic trust evolves; withdrawal is promoted by basic mistrust.

Autonomy versus shame/doubt is the second psychosocial crisis that is presented during toddlerhood. The toddler is engaged in a sense of discovery, trying to express individuality as an autonomous and equal being in the world. If the toddler is able to learn that there are things in the environment that are dependable and situations that allow for the assertion of independence, then confidence and autonomy are integrated into the personality. If independence is discouraged by the environment or parents, the young child learns to doubt or to have shame concerning independent action.

The third stage of development involves the psychosocial crisis of *initiative versus guilt*. Occurring in early childhood, the individual is involved in the initial exploration of the social and physical world. If the child experiments in the social and physical environment with success, then a sense of accomplishment and a desire for an initiative for further experimentation is developed. When experimentation is discouraged or even punished, the child integrates guilt into the personality. Initiative enables the child to build a sense of purpose, while guilt promotes inhibitions. As the child reaches school age, the crisis of *industry versus inferiority* is confronted. Industry develops as a result of the child's learning to master the environment and the social skills that society expects. Industry lends itself to a sense of individual competence. If competition and the pressure of mastering the environment or social skills become too great, the child develops a sense of inferiority because of his or her inability to achieve or succeed.

As the child moves into adolescence, the crisis of *identity versus role confusion* occurs. This is when young people either begin to assimilate the roles, values, and concepts of the parents into a modified version for themselves, or when they become confused, unable to reach a conclusion about identity. Fidelity to one's self is the goal of this stage. *Intimacy versus isolation* is the sixth psychosocial crisis and it occurs in young adulthood. Here, individuals struggle to establish the life strength of love. They either develop close and intimate relationships with people, or they isolate themselves, unable to share their identity and self.

The middle adulthood crisis is *generativity versus stagnation*. Care for the next generation is the central theme of this stage. Those who are able to establish themselves as guides and caretakers to the younger generation will express this generativity. Those who become absorbed in their own personal needs and interests become stagnated.

Finally, the late adulthood psychosocial crisis is *integrity versus despair*. Individuals in this stage struggle to find the wisdom and to define the meaning of their lives, having passed through the previous seven stages.

As individuals in the family develop, each will have different motivations and experiences that have been shaped during the psychosocial crises. Each family member's development and experience, in turn, has an effect on how the entire family develops and relates. Therefore, understanding the strivings and motivations of the individuals promotes the therapist's knowledge of how the family relates when it faces the aging task.

Family or Systemic Transactional Patterns

This systemic dimension deals with the communication or interaction patterns in relationships (Boszormenyi-Nagy & Krasner, 1986). These objectifiable transactions produce organization or laws that define power alignments, structure, and belief systems.

In classical systemic family therapy, the symptom or dysfunction of the family is seen as being maintained by the behavior of the system. In other words, dysfunction is created in order to ensure the functioning or survival of the family system. For example, in a family where the father becomes depressed over his unhappy career or marriage, there can be a son who might be prompted to act out in some fashion. If the son suddenly starts failing in school and skipping classes, the father must focus his attention on the son, dealing with the child in a competent manner. Thus the son's symptomatology maintains the father's functioning and so preserves the system.

This kind of system maintenance also is seen in aging families.

For instance, an older widow was very dependent on her son. The widow saw that he was grieving over his wife, who was dying. Concerned for her son and also frightened for herself, the mother developed a symptom that required the son to put his grief "on hold." In the retirement facility where the mother lived, she periodically spat on the floors of public sitting and dining areas. The son came to the facility where he would plead with his mother not to spit in these places. The son functioned in a competent caretaking manner, although his own grief was neglected, and the family system was essentially maintained. (This case is reviewed in full in Chapter 7.)

Systemic transactions and behaviors tend to define how the family operates in terms of power and hierarchy. For instance, it is not uncommon in family therapy to see one person serve as the "communicator" for the family. In these types of systems, the person either speaks directly for other members or the members check with the communicator for approval. This type of structure reinforces that the family communicator is the most powerful person in the family. Transactions then move along in a prescribed way.

Another way transactions tend to define power and hierarchy is through coalitions. For instance, a mother tries to enforce a curfew with her adolescent daughter. However, the mother may be unsuccessful because the father either openly supports the daughter's position by playing a "peacemaker" role between the two, or by passive withdrawal from the system. The father's actions in both cases tend to define the daughter's position as being equal in power to that of the mother. The father, unwilling to form an alliance with the mother, forms a coalition with the daughter, thus defeating or neutralizing the mother's actions.

Power alignments and coalitions are also important in aging families. For instance, an older divorced father, who engaged in several regrettable activities when his children were growing up, was depressed. He tried to effect a reconciliation. Some of the children formed a coalition, refusing to accept any effort the father made to apologize for the past. The coalition essentially kept the father in the scapegoat position, continuing to define family problems as stemming solely from him. The father was powerless; the system remained the same.

Systemic family therapists utilize a variety of techniques designed to change the transactions or behavior in the family; they aim to help the system develop more useful power alignments and belief structures. Family systems theory is very positive in its orientation that the family—not the therapist—is able to adapt itself to more functional ways of relating. Therefore, the therapist is to be the initiator who helps the family change old patterns. Among the more notable structural and strategic therapies (e.g., Minuchin & Fishman, 1981; Madanes, 1984; Haley, 1987), metaphors, restructuring, relabeling, paradoxes, reframing, blocking, positioning, and prescribing are some of the techniques used to bring about change in the system.

For any therapist who is involved with families, the value of systemic transactions in defining the family and perpetuating old structures and belief systems is evident. The therapist needs techniques that help the family address second-order changes and modify dysfunctional patterns. From a contextual therapy view, however, this dimension alone does not address some of the ethical concerns of the family. In other words, behavior by members of the system has a component of care, balance, fairness, and concern for the intergenerational group. This component is defined by contextual therapy as the *relational ethics* dimension. Techniques that concentrate on changing behavior and transactions without giving consideration to this subjective ethical component may damage the family.

Relational Ethics

The three dimensions just mentioned are familiar to the mental health community. It is the fourth dimension, relational ethics, that sets the contextual approach apart from other therapies, and is the real contribution of contextual therapy to understanding the family therapy field.

The dimension of relational ethics deals with the subjective balance of trustworthiness, justice, loyalty, merit, and entitlement between members of a relationship. As members of the relationship interact in an interdependent fashion, relational ethics requires them to assume responsibility for consequences and strive for fairness and equity in the process of give and take (Hargrave, Jennings, & Anderson, 1991). Although the four dimensions in the contextual approach are inseparable from each other, Boszormenyi-Nagy and Krasner (1986) believe that it is the mobilization of the resources in this dimension that constitutes the most important factor in healing dysfunctional relationships in therapy. Despite its significance, this fourth dimension has received little previous attention in psychological research (Van Heusden & Van Den Eerenbeemt, 1987).

Relational ethics is initially rooted in the philosophy of Martin Buber (1958), who believed that individuals depend on relationship to experience self-understanding and self-delineation. In other words, for individuals to have a sufficient basis to experience emotions and thoughts, they are dependent on the experience of relating, giving, and receiving from another person. Relational ethics is also based on an innate sense of justice or fairness that exists within people (Boszormenyi-Nagy & Krasner, 1986). This innate sense demands that there be balance between what an individual is entitled to receive from the relationship and what he or she is obligated to give to maintain the relationship. Simply stated, relational ethics is a relational demand that persons maintain a fair balance and equity between what they are entitled to take and what they are obligated to give to relationships.

This balance of obligation (give) and merit (take) can be envisioned as a ledger of the relationship. In Figure 3.1 a relationship ledger between a husband and wife is represented. On the left side of the ledger is the merit that the individual is entitled to receive from the spouse, either because of heritage or because the individual has fulfilled and met expected obligations. For instance, a husband may be entitled to receive respect, care, and spousal

ENTITLEMENT	OBLIGATION
(individual is entitled to)	(individual is expected to)
1. Respect	1. Respect
2. Care	2. Care
3. Intimacy	3. Intimacy

Figure 3.1. Example of a Spousal Relationship Ledger

intimacy from his wife. He is entitled to these things because these elements form a part of the marital arrangement, but most important, he is entitled because he does those things for his wife. She, in turn, is obligated to reciprocate. On the right side of the ledger are the obligations that the husband is required to fulfill in order to maintain the relationship. His obligation to his wife is the same as his entitlement from his wife. The relationship is balanced and fair, as each spouse symmetrically gives to the other.

Relational ethics exists in two types of relationships (Van Heusden & Van Den Eerenbeemt, 1987). First, the ethical dimension exists in *horizontal* relationships between partners of equal positions who have a mutual obligation to and expectation from each other, such as spouses, siblings, and friends. In these relationships, fairness is maintained by symmetrical balance between the give and take. As in the previous example, the husband–wife relationship contains the mutual expectation of respect, care, and intimacy. If one spouse does not fulfill the obligation, the relationship becomes unfair and begins to break down.

Relational ethics also exists in *vertical* relationships. These relationships are between succeeding generations, such as parents and children. Although fair and just, they are, by definition, asymmetrical in give and take. Figure 3.2 offers an example of a relationship ledger between a parent and an infant where the parent has much more obligation than the child. The left side of the ledger shows

ENTITLEMENT	OBLIGATION
(individual is entitled to)	*(individual is expected to)*
1. Love	1. Growth/Response
2. Care	
3. Nurture	
4. Security	
5. Protection	
6. Discipline	

Figure 3.2.   Example of a Parent–Child Relationship Ledger

that the parent is obligated to provide love, care, nurturing, security, protection, and discipline (among other things). However, the
only entitlement or merit that the parent really receives from the
child is the child's response, most often growth. At first glance,
this may seem an extremely imbalanced and an unfair relationship
to the parent.

It is necessary to view the ledger from an intergenerational perspective. From this view, the relationship is asymmetrical but fair,
because the parent was once an infant and was the recipient of the
same love, care, nurturing, security, protection, and discipline that he
or she now gives to an infant. By fulfilling the obligation for such care
to the infant, the parent earns merit by obligating the child to pass
along such care to his or her future children. In vertical relationships,
balance and fairness are maintained down through the succeeding
generations. When individuals responsibly fulfill their obligations,
they essentially empower the next generation to do the same; this
enhances family existence and mutual caring.

When individuals have relationships (whether vertical or horizontal) that are balanced between giving what the relationship
requires and receiving what each person is entitled to receive, then

the innate sense of fairness or justice is satisfied (Boszormenyi-Nagy & Krasner, 1980). As this balance between give and take continues over time, the people involved in the relationship learn to trust each other. As trust builds, the partners are enabled to give to one another. In other words, those in trustworthy relationships believe that the other will give the entitlement that each one deserves without having to be manipulated or threatened with retribution. Both are free to give because each trusts the other to give (Boszormenyi-Nagy & Krasner, 1986). Therefore, a balance of give and take in a relationship over a period of time satisfies each individual's sense of trust and justice (Van Heusden & Van Den Eerenbeemt, 1987).

Reserves of trust seem to accrue in relationships. Let us say the wife becomes incapacitated for an extended time because of an illness. She might not be able to fulfill the obligation of providing responsible care and intimacy to her husband. The burden of care might fall entirely on the husband. However, if the couple has years of balanced and fair relations behind them, it is most likely that the husband will gladly fulfill the extra obligation. He will trust that if and when she is able, the wife will work toward reestablishing the balanced relationship. Further, he trusts that the wife would do the same for him if the roles were reversed. However, if the reserve of trust does not exist, the potential of the husband's providing care for the wife while receiving nothing in return becomes more tentative.

When there is an imbalance or injustice in the relationship ledger of give and take, dysfunction often occurs (Boszormenyi-Nagy & Spark, 1984). Persons who do not receive care, nurturing, and love from a relationship often will seek a replacement for these emotions. However, they will probably do so in a destructive manner (Boszormenyi-Nagy & Krasner, 1986). In other words, individuals know what they are entitled to. When they do not receive their entitlement, they do not forget about it—they move to get what they deserve for themselves, using threats, manipulation, or even more dysfunctional behavior. This behavior is called *destruc-*

tive entitlement; it is the individual's claim to self-justifying compensation on the relational ledger. Destructive entitlement can manifest itself in many ways, including paranoid attitudes, hostility, emotional cutoffs, and destructive behavior (Boszormenyi-Nagy & Krasner, 1986). When this imbalance occurs over a long period, extensive distrust develops in relationships. Where there is a lack of trust, individuals refuse to give to each other because they believe that it will deplete their resources. They receive nothing in return.

In the intergenerational family, it is apparent that the ledger of entitlements and obligations is complex. In vertical relationships, individuals in a family inherit a legacy of either balanced, fair, and trustworthy relationships or imbalanced, unfair, and untrustworthy relationships (Boszormenyi-Nagy, 1987). As we have seen in the previous example of the parent and infant, the parent who fulfills obligations empowers the infant one day to pass along the fair exchange of giving. However, if the parent has experienced an injustice, he or she will be driven to compensate for this violation (Boszormenyi-Nagy & Spark, 1984). For instance, if the parent does not provide the infant with love, care, nurturing, and protection, the infant will not receive these essentials. Where the parent does not provide proper care, the parent begins to expect the growing child to fulfill these emotional needs. The child, as children do, tries to comply. Essentially, however, the parent is asking the child to meet adult obligations, while not empowering the child with the entitlement the child deserves.

Inevitably, the child fails to supply the parent with what the parent feels he or she deserves. The parent might become more manipulative and demanding, and possibly abusive, in an effort to get the child to fulfill the "obligation." The parent does this because he or she feels justified in demanding that his or her deserved entitlement of love, care, and nurturing—not met long ago when he or she was a child—be met by his or her own child. And there is a good possibility that as a child, the parent was expected to try to fulfill these "obligations" toward his or her own parents. This is an intense cycle of loyalty and entitlement; it originates in past generations and is passed along in a slate of distrust and injustice (Boszormenyi-Nagy & Spark, 1984).

Boszormenyi-Nagy feels that this dimension is the location of the emotional field of the family. Any therapeutic change must include consideration of relational ethics in order to be successful (personal communication, October 14, 1988). Relational ethics governs individual and family actions in relationships, demanding that merits be sought and obligations be met.

The ethical dimension of a three-, four-, or five-generation aging family becomes quite important. For the first time in history, these complex intergenerational families in our society must explore new balances in obligations and responsibilities to one another. For middle-aged adults, there are questions of responsibility and obligations toward their aging parents. For younger adults, there are questions concerning entitlement as they see their parents struggle with the relationship and care of their grandparents. Finally, older adults must deal with the stress of being over-benefitted by some relationships. They sense that they are a burden to care for; they wonder how they can continue to contribute to the family. Overshadowing these relational concerns are the larger intergenerational ledger concerns. Unresolved issues of the past and emotionally charged relationships once again resurface, as the family is forced to deal with issues of aging. For example, an older family member may expect his or her adult children to provide the same care that he or she gave to elderly parents. The adult children may see this time as their last opportunity to receive from the older person the nurturing or validation they did not receive in the past (Anderson & Hargrave, 1990).

THE CONTEXTUAL FRAMEWORK IN THE
LAST STAGE OF LIFE

The intergenerational approach of contextual therapy seems appropriate to apply to aging families because of the integration of the four dimensions. The dimension of *facts* takes into account the tremendous daily difficulties that face the aging family—health, living situation, care, and finances. The dimension of *family and systemic transactions* reminds the therapist of how power alignments and communication patterns may present persistent problems in the family. The dimensions of *individual psychology* and *relational ethics* seem to be especially important when dealing with an aging family.

In psychosocial development, the last life crisis presented is integrity versus despair. At this time of life, there is a natural reminiscing about one's life. The individual deals with the reality that most of life is behind, with death lying just ahead (Butler, 1963). It is at this point that the relational ethics dimension is essential to understanding aging families. If there is a balanced, trustworthy ethic in the intergenerational family, the older person will be able to empower younger family members with the wisdom of the years. Physical deterioration that accompanies aging will be seen as a natural process; emphasis will switch from what the older person was once able to do to what he or she is still able to do. The older person will develop a sense of shifting power and importance to the next generation. The family will accept these gifts, recognizing the profound lessons that their elders have to share, and knowing that the legacy of the elder will live through the coming generations. In short, the older person and his or her family experience integrity as they have lived life in a trustworthy fashion, developing the delicate shifting balance between relational give and take. Relational ethics addresses this emotional field of the aging intergenerational family so essential to living life well.

However, some older people will look back at this crucial time and be filled with regret over lost experiences, unaccomplished goals, and harm done to family and others. The family ledger will be significantly imbalanced. Manipulation and symptomatology that may have only surfaced in the family in younger years may now become exaggerated; the older person

INTEGRITY ... v e r s u s ... D E S P A I R	
Individuals have a process orientation to life and usually achieve successful balance between give and take.	Individuals have a result orientation to life and may experience frustration of justice imbalance.
Entitlements Obligations	**Entitlements Obligations**
The individual achieves balance by oscillation of give and take and reciprocity.	The individual achieves imbalance, which may lead to symptomatic or dysfunctional behavior.

Figure 3.3. Relational Ethics in the Last Stage of Life

and the family sense that time is running out on the opportunity to gain entitlement and fulfill obligations. Instead of wisdom, the older person will be filled with regret and despair. Family members will focus on physical and mental deterioration, as repeated efforts are made to find a "cure" for the decline. Rather than confronting the necessary adaption that aging requires, old roles and patterns will be held onto tenaciously by the family. The family will grow weary of the process and find their emotional resources drained. The passing of the older person will come as a relief.

Each stage of psychosocial development and the family life cycle carries with it a set of individual entitlements and family obligations. As illustrated in Figure 3.3, the members of a family that are able to balance these obligations and entitlements are usually process oriented in meeting one another's needs. Families of this type are likely to produce older people who develop integrity and wisdom in the last stage of life. Families that are unable to balance individual entitlements and family obligations are usually result oriented; they seek only to secure their own entitlement. Older people in these families are likely to come to the end of life feeling only hopelessness and despair.

THE THERAPEUTIC PROCESS OF CONTEXTUAL THERAPY

Boszormenyi-Nagy and Ulrich (1981) define the goal of contextual therapy as the movement of the family toward *rejunctive* efforts to balance the intergenerational ledger in acceptable and helpful ways. In other words, relational integrity is achieved as the family members make constructive efforts to balance give and take. As the family achieves this balance, family members begin to develop trust in the relationships once again. As trust builds in the family, it acts as a resource to empower the family to promote the fair balance of give and take (Boszormenyi-Nagy, 1979).

Symptoms or dysfunctions in the family are generally viewed as an expression of an underlying imbalance in intergenerational relationships. Therefore, the contextual therapist usually shifts concerns away from the presenting problems fairly quickly, allowing family members to express their entitlement concerns individually (Kaslow, 1987). The therapist then explores in depth the multilateral nature of the individual concerns (Boszormenyi-Nagy & Ulrich, 1981). Every individual family member has an interest in each family issue; the therapist seeks to understand all viewpoints and then takes turns siding with each family member. This surfacing of concerns and siding with members—called *multidirectional partiality*—is the primary therapeutic tool in the contextual approach (Boszormenyi-Nagy & Krasner, 1986). The process of therapy involves the following: to speak openly and negotiate ledger issues; to explore loyalty and legacy issues in the family; to undo family and relational stagnation; to examine cutoffs or disjunctive efforts in the family; and to examine relational corruption or destructive entitlement in the family (Boszormenyi-Nagy & Ulrich, 1981).

CONCLUSION

Some families handle the process and stress of aging well; others do not. Several factors determine how a family faces problems. Families that are process oriented are probably unlikely to seek therapy unless it is for specific situational stress. Most aging families that will seek therapy will be locked into the despair of long-standing imbalances. These are the families that need help to finish well. The therapist with the aging family has the goal to make the ending better than the beginning and middle. Finishing well for these families means more positive beginnings for the future generations.

II

THE BEGINNING STAGES OF THERAPY

4

THE BEGINNING OF THERAPY

We began our clinical research at the small personal care facility to explore how to help older people, as well as their families, overcome despair and dysfunction in the last stages of their lives. However, the reality of helping older people and their families is very different from the lofty goals set in the comfort of one's own office. These were lovely people, but there were problems that were quite severe and caveats in doing therapy with these aging families.

First, there were the sometimes overwhelming health problems and medical concerns. Some clients had trouble walking and caring for themselves because of bone or muscle deterioration, which prompted the practical concern of just being able to meet with the older person. Some were simply not able to come to an office, much less negotiate stairs or elevators. Most clients had moderate to substantial hearing loss. This presented quite a challenge in attempting to make sure the older person had heard the message without undermining his or her self-esteem by constantly shouting and repeating statements or questions. Besides common aches and pains associated with aging, some of the people had terminal illnesses or medical problems that caused great pain. Therapy with these people often took place when they were in physical pain, making concentration very difficult. This usually meant that therapy sessions had to be shorter than is ideal. Vision limitations, effects of medication and overmedication, and tremors all were a part of dealing with the health problems of this population.

Second, there were memory difficulties. Some of the people had quite severe organic brain deterioration. We had questions about whether these people could be helped to overcome despair if they could not make sense of the messages that were going to the brain. Most of the older people had at least some short-term memory loss. Many therapy sessions would cover the same ground several times, as the older person recounted the same story.

Third, there were the barriers to family therapy, as the intergenerational aging family is often spread out across the United States. Most of the responsibility and family interaction fell to one adult child or caretaker, who lived closest to the older person. There were questions of whom to involve in therapy and how to deal with the ramifications of only having part of the intergenerational group available.

These were just a few of the initial concerns we had when we started doing therapy with aging families. Older people and aging families are just people and families, but they do present therapeutic challenges that are different from those in a younger group. The purpose of this chapter is to present an overview of the therapeutic process and then some particulars of beginning therapy with the aging family.

OVERVIEW OF THE THERAPEUTIC PROCESS

The contextual framework is essential to understanding the goals of therapy with aging families. Although there may be certain types of situational stresses, such as time-management, financial, or coping issues, we view the relational dimension or the emotional field of the individual and the family as the root of most symptomatology or dysfunction. Therefore, the first and primary goal in therapy, like contextual therapy, is to help move the aging family toward rejunctive efforts to balance the intergenerational ledger of individual entitlements and family obligations.

Therapeutic Goals with Aging Families

It is always necessary to recognize the psychological reality that exists for each person, and it is especially so with aging families. Although there are many individual and relational aspects to this reality, there are two primary issues that aging families must come to grips with in order to finish well. First, aging families must deal with the psychological and relational stress associated with loss. Adjusting to the economic, physical, and emotional losses in old age presents a profound obstacle to the family. Emotional losses entail much more than losing a person; they also involve losing relationships. Carl Whitaker made this clear at a marriage and family therapy meeting, when he stated that as much as he would miss his wife if she died, he would miss what they were together much more. Aging families must deal with deaths of spouses, friends, parents, grandparents, and great-grandparents. Much more than a reduction in the number of family members, these losses are multiple reductions in "us" relationships, which affect all members.

Specific losses move the family to the realization of ultimate loss—letting go of life. To negotiate this loss well, the older individual and family have to see that there is a spiritual transcendence long after physical life is terminated. This transcendence exists in the intergenerational linkage that the family has perpetuated for centuries. The older person has now done his or her part to perpetuate the family for generations to come. Refusal to deal with these losses means denial, futility, and sometimes extreme efforts to hold on. The first goal of therapy, then, is to help the older person and the family let go.

The second therapeutic goal is to help members of the aging family reconcile themselves with the past. Even in healthy families, such reconciliation takes place as older individuals and their families take stock of lost opportunities, hurts, and regrets that occurred during the life cycle. But aging families usually take part in this activity willingly. Despairing older people and symptomatic or dysfunctional families either refuse to look at these past issues or find it too difficult to deal with the past. As we have seen, however, the intergenerational ledger keeps the past alive in future generations. Therefore, older people and aging families need to communicate about, reconcile with, and forgive the past. In this way, groundwork is laid for trustworthy relations in the intergenerational family.

The Stages of Therapy with the Aging Family

We believe that the intergenerational ledger concept of the relational ethics dimension of contextual therapy is the best framework within which to address these two goals in therapy. However, we also believe that working with aging families involves the use of specific techniques. Although the contextual framework and the intergenerational ledger are used to organize and conceptualize family issues and problems, we also have integrated techniques from other therapies to facilitate the trust-building in the family. We have integrated these techniques to cover three broad stages of therapy with aging families: *life validation*, *life review*, and *therapeutic interventions*. Again, each stage is used within the contextual framework and is aimed at the rejunctive effort of balancing obligations and entitlements at the last stage of life.

Life validation.

The beginning stage of therapy is called life validation (Asnes, 1983). In general, the therapist uses a general macrohistorical knowledge of events to gain access to the older person's microhistorical perspective on his or her life. These initial sessions, usually with only the older person, give the therapist the opportunity to join with the elderly client. As this person talks about his or her individual history and perspective on development, the therapist has the opportunity to give credit and to be partial in recognizing the client's background, history, and contribution.

When the therapist takes this position of initial validation, the older person recognizes the therapist as an advocate; trust is formulated in the therapeutic relationship. The life-validation stage also gives the therapist a chance to access the intergenerational family relationship ledger from the older individual's developmental perspective. Usually, this first stage of therapy will last one or two sessions.

It is amazing how ageism has affected the professional therapeutic community in our society. It is not unusual for professional therapists to direct their conversation about the problems of the older person to the adult children. Often, conversation with the older person is patronizing and inappropriate for adults. Butler (1975) hypothesized that this effect of ageism on the professional community stems from individuals attempting to avoid the personal reality of aging and death. Perhaps therapists feel discomfort in joining with and talking to the older person because they have never been around older people. At any rate, life validation presents the therapist and the older person with a place to begin that is common to both, and it helps facilitate a meaningful and therapeutic relationship. The technique of life validation is discussed in detail in the next chapter.

Life review.

One of the most influential therapies with older people, and certainly the best researched, is life review (Butler, 1963). As a person approaches death and reckons with personal vulnerability—at any age—a universal process of reminiscing occurs. Life review in older people may result in greater self-awareness and wisdom or in excessive guilt, agitation, and despair. The review and reminiscence process seems to be especially intense around areas of past conflicts, regrettable choices, or hurts inflicted on others.

From a contextual perspective, the second stage of therapy (life review) provides the therapist with insight into the intergenerational family-ledger issues. Although the life review process can be done with just the older person, important details can be given by the entire family. Having the family present offers two benefits: First, as the older person talks of the past and the family understands, entitlement is earned; responsible and reciprocal interactions take place. This enhances trust in the family. Second, as the family interacts about the past, it clarifies not only ledger issues, but also systemic or transactional patterns in the family. Life review gives the therapist another opportunity to credit and be partial to family members, but the information in this stage of therapy is much more detailed than that of the life-validation stage. Conflicts are clarified and resources are strengthened during this stage. The therapist is enabled to begin to hypothesize about family-ledger imbalances and to look for specific points of therapeutic intervention. The length of this middle stage of therapy varies, but most often it lasts between two and six sessions. The technique of life review is discussed in detail in Chapter 6.

Interventions.

After trust and resources are strengthened in the aging family, the therapist moves the family into the third stage of therapy, intervention. This stage lasts until the family therapy is terminated. The key element in constructing interventions is the ability of the therapist to encourage and coach the family to use its relational resources to address the imbalances in the ethical dimension. Therefore, armed with the knowledge of family-ledger imbalances gained in the stages of life validation and life review, the therapist suggests interventions that will correct imbalances and build additional trust and resource in the family.

It is important to realize that when interventions are successful, the problems associated with aging do not dissipate. As we have seen, aging presents a variety of problems with which both strong and weak families must deal. Interventions are designed to relieve symptomatology and dysfunction. In addition, they are designed to strengthen the family so that the intergenerational group can deal successfully with the stresses and tasks that are ahead. Therefore, interventions are not simple problem-solving approaches, but rather are endeavors to enhance the family resources so that finishing life well can be accomplished. Various intervention strategies are discussed in Part III.

THE ROLE OF THE THERAPIST

In most cases, it is the adult children of the older person who will make initial contact about therapy. The motivation to seek help for the older person is stimulated by problems that may be related to depression, anxiety, sleep disorders, disorientation, stagnation, stress, grief, symptomatology, or regret. The literature notes that the current cohort of older people is not inclined to take a positive view of counseling. It was our expectation that therapy would be resisted by older people. However, contrary to our expectation, every older person who had an adult child or caretaker contact us about therapy agreed to participate. There was very little resistance to therapy from the family, and when it did exist, it was usually a sibling of the adult child who expressed misgivings.

The first question about the role of the therapist is what position he or she should assume with the family. The therapist first and foremost should be an advocate for all the generations and individuals in the family—whether they are present or not. One of the initial ways this is accomplished is to offer respect for each generational position. Here, we feel the age of the therapist is important. An older therapist can offer respect to the different generations and individual positions because of his or her similar experiences. In essence, this therapist has been through the life cycle and can naturally identify and support individuals in the family at particular life stages. For the younger therapist, the task of offering respect is quite different. It is not unusual for a therapist to be 50 or 60 years younger than the member of the oldest generation. Although the younger therapist cannot offer similar experience, he or she still can maintain a powerful therapeutic position.

First, whenever possible, the therapist should allow the older person to be the teacher when it comes to his or her life. Even the most despairing older adult has had a tremendous life experience. Allowing the older person and the family to teach and to recall these periods represents an acknowledgement of that person's wisdom of years. Second, it is essential to listen to descriptions of the situation and stories of the family without reframing or giving alternate meanings. The family tells the story in a certain way because it is a reflection of the relational ethics dimension and the family ledger. To reframe or try to change meaning violates the family members' perception of their relationships. Third, the therapist should address all of the adults in the room as equals. This approach models for the family the fact that even though the therapist may be young, he or she is able to relate at an adult level to each adult generation. This component not only helps the older generations to recognize the contributions of the therapist, but it also is important for the younger adults who will witness, perhaps for the first time, how to take adult positions with older family members. A common mistake of therapists working with older people for the first time is that they talk to them as if they do not understand everyday language. When the therapist makes this type of mistake, he or she supports the power of one generation over another and is disrespectful to the individual interests of other family members. During the initial stages of therapy, the therapist should be the one who is being taught as he or she assesses the relational dimension and builds trust in the therapeutic interactions. Simply stated, the therapist listens well and is willing to be taught by the family, but maintains an equal adult position in the family and expects all adults to maintain similar positions.

During the middle stage of therapy, the advocacy role of the therapist shifts slightly in emphasis from one of being taught to one that includes more overt partiality toward individual family members and a commentator role on family interaction and relational issues. As family members begin to realize that their individual issues will be credited by the therapist, they become more willing to listen and to credit other members' issues. Therefore, the overt partiality shown by the therapist serves as a model of giving and trust for the family. As the therapist comments on family interaction and relational issues, the family is encouraged to explore its own resources in addressing some of the problems in the family.

During the intervention stage of therapy with aging families, the role of the therapist shifts to that of an intergenerational coach. Although there clearly are interventions and directives suggested by the contextual therapist, the interventions that we are discussing here are much more directive and may require more involvement by the therapist. We suggest more directive coaching by the therapist during interventions than is usually found in the contextual approach for two primary reasons. First, the intergenerational aging family interacts much like a disengaged family (Minuchin, 1974); that is, family members are not as involved in day-to-day activities with each other. However, in an aging family, this usually is not due to impenetrable or rigid boundaries, although these may also exist, but simply results because the intergenerational family members seldom live together.

This lack of interaction and time together to work things out makes it difficult for the family to explore new relational options. Often, the therapy session will be the longest period the family spends together at one time. These families simply need more direction from the therapist.

Second, there is the element of time. Most aging families have had imbalanced relational issues for decades, and discovering new options may be difficult without the therapist's suggesting new methods of intervention. In addition, there is the inherent time limit presented to the aging family—mortality. The oldest gen-

eration cannot realistically expect to have a decade or even several
years to explore trustworthy relations. As a directive coach, the
therapist can help the family address old wounds faster and point
clearly to new balances of family interactions.

While the therapist is in this directive coaching role, he or she
must be cautious. Interventions are not formulated on the basis
of simple symptom removal; but rather are designed with the balance of the intergenerational relational ethics ledger in mind. It
is essential that the therapist be as precise as possible in assessing
the relational reality for the family. He or she must be careful not
to direct interventions that will violate individual family member's
interests. Of course, no therapist ever really knows the "whole
story" involved in the relational reality of a family, so the coaching
therapist must be flexible and understanding while helping the
family to change.

There are certainly more concerns in doing therapy with a family whose eldest member is 85 than in doing therapy with one in
which the eldest member is 40. For example, therapists must be
sensitive about room lighting when an older person who might
have faulty eyesight is involved. By the same token, many older
people have hearing problems and so the therapist must speak
clearly and sufficiently loudly. If older clients wear hearing aids,
other noises such as those from air conditioners and fans must
be kept to a minimum. Even the sitting area must be considered.
Having firm, slightly elevated, but comfortable seats shows sensitivity to the older person.

Perhaps one of the greatest concerns of therapy with older adults
has to do with organic brain deterioration or memory loss. Indeed,
it is difficult to work with an aging family if the eldest member
cannot remember the last session or even why he or she is in the
therapist's office. We have several suggestions here to enhance the
memory capacity of older people in therapy. The first suggestion
is to slow down the pace of the therapy session slightly. Therapists
should monitor the pace of their talking to give the maximum
opportunity for the older person's brain to encode the messages.

This slowing down does not mean that therapists have to become more demonstrative or louder in their communication; the session is simply slower. Second, it is helpful if the therapist makes frequent summary statements during the session. These statements should build as the session lengthens to include three to five summary statements by the end of the session. Therapists should use the same wording when providing the summary statements and the summaries should be offered often, as they will serve as memory prompts to the older person and other family members.

Third, therapists may have greater success in helping older clients remember the therapy sessions if the scheduling of appointments is more concentrated. We have found the most effective method of helping older adults remember therapy to be scheduling sessions two or three times a week instead of the traditional once a week. We also have had more success when sessions were slightly shorter than one hour—about 40 to 50 minutes.

THE THERAPIST'S FAMILY-OF-ORIGIN ISSUES

Any good therapist knows the dangers of countertransference, or the reexperiencing of feelings on the therapist's part in response to a clinical family (Whitaker, 1982). This can lead the therapist to have distorted feelings toward individuals or the family as a whole. For instance, if a therapist grew up in a family where a father was distant and neglectful, the therapist may be especially hostile to a family with an emotionally uninvolved father. If a therapist had a domineering parent who still has an undue amount of influence in the therapist's life, he or she may be hesitant to have an adult-to-adult relationship with a domineering client. Countertransference is always an issue in therapy, but it is especially salient in therapy with aging families because there are so many roles and developmental stages being explored simultaneously by the therapist. The relational reality of the family is complex enough without the therapist's inserting his or her own intergenerational ledger issues into therapy. Countertransference can lead to bad therapeutic judgment, but it can also be damaging to the family, because a therapist may be partial to one individual or generation at the expense of another.

On this issue, the therapist must also model responsibility. In our opinion, a good therapist not only knows what his or her own family-of-origin issues are, but also is willing to deal with them in a responsible manner. It is indeed difficult for therapists to encourage a family to build intergenerational trust when they themselves are emotionally cut off from their own parents. Most families, including therapists' families, have intergenerational ledger issues. If a therapist is willing to work on balancing these issues with his or her own family, then the issues are more overt and less likely to seep covertly into the therapist's perception of a clinical family.

Related to this issue is the therapist's feelings about aging, death, and dying. We live in a society that largely shuns the idea of aging and death and is primarily focused on young and middle adulthood (Butler, 1975). It would be hard to imagine that a therapist could help a family deal with the grief and resolution of life losses that aging prompts, if he or she did not see aging and death as an appropriate and beneficial part of the life cycle. In short, the therapist must not ignore his or her apprehension about old age and must gain an appreciation for what aging means to the family.

ASSESSMENT OF THE AGING FAMILY

Assessment is the key to discovering the relational resources necessary to construct good interventions that will help the family build trustworthy relations through intergenerational balance. However, it is important to remember that assessment is a continuing activity throughout the therapy process. The therapist should assess the family and have initial "hunches," but these should be held tentatively and should be modified as therapy proceeds. Since there are four dimensions to the relational reality of the aging family system, assessment should proceed through these four organizing factors.

Assessment of Facts

Facts are objectifiable realities that have affected the relational reality of the family. Some facts may be changeable, such as medical conditions, and some may be irreversible, such as growing up in an adoptive family. No matter what the facts are, it is important that the therapist assess and give fair consideration to how various facts have shaped the family.

Medical facts constitute the most common assessment done for older people in our society. Indeed, these facts are important, because they will have a great impact on how the individual feels about himself or herself and how the rest of the family interacts. For instance, if an older person cannot walk or does not have the manual dexterity necessary to dress, this affects his or her ability to maintain an positive self-image and that will have an impact on the family as well as other social relationships.

Cognitive assessment of the older person is also necessary. Although there are elaborate procedures for psychological assessment of an individual's cognitive status, we are essentially interested in memory and affect. An older person may have Alzheimer's disease or organic brain syndrome, but if it is in an early or moderate stage, the person will still have access to some memory and have quite dynamic affect. Some questions therapists should ask themselves while assessing cognitive status are as follows:

1. What kind of memory does the older person have? Is it short-term memory (a few minutes to three days) or long-term memory?
2. If the older person does not recognize times, places, and peo-

ple, does it interfere with his or her self-image and expression of emotion?

3. If the older person does not recognize times, places, and people, does it hinder his or her ability to take care of such basic functions as eating, sleeping, and personal hygiene?
4. If the older person is experiencing illusions or hallucinations, are they of a nature that is dangerous to the older person or others?
5. If the older person is experiencing illusions or hallucinations, is it a metaphor about emotional turmoil that is going on in the individual's psychology?

It is difficult to work with aging families in which an older person has extreme dementia. However, if there is enough cognitive capacity left in the older person to access helpful emotions, we believe therapy is feasible. Many older people have an "emotional" memory that may enable them to address ledger and family concerns, even though they may not remember specific incidents. Making restitution in ledger imbalances has often made a difference in the behavior and affect of an older person, even though many times he or she did not remember the specific therapy session where the restitution took place. This is a new area, but we believe that it is better to try therapy with the cognitively impaired than to do nothing.

One of the more essential areas of assessments is to know the medications and physical condition of the older person. Most older people seek medical advice from a variety of physicians for numerous physical ailments and family members are usually very supportive in seeking such help in dealing with their elder member. In many cases, the various physicians will prescribe medications for these conditions. Thus it is not unusual for an older person to be taking several medications for an array of ailments for years at a time, and sometimes the prescribing physicians are not aware of the full medication regime of the person. Many older people, therefore, are overmedicated; some medications actually work against the conditions that other medications are meant to correct. Also, some medications will cause extreme behavior in older people, such as depression, hallucinations, and tremors. It is important for the therapist to assess the effects of the medication regime and work with the physicians and the family to medicate the older person only when it is necessary and helpful. Up to 43 percent of older people misuse drugs in some way (Raffoul, Cooper, & Love, 1981). No amount of therapy will cure anxiety or depression if the cause of the problem is in the form of daily medication.

Psychotropic medication should be prescribed with extreme caution. Chambers, White, Lindquist and Harter (1987) report that most of these medications simply have not been tested in their effects on the older population. The older brain reacts differently to psychotropic medication than does a middle-age brain. Prolonged use can potentially have catastrophic results in causing brain damage. Wolfe, Fugate, Hulstrand, and Kamimoto (1988) report that most older people are given either wrong medications, dosages that are too high, or medications whose risks outweigh their benefits.

However, not all of the facts that require assessment are of a medical nature. The therapist must also be sensitive to the circumstances that have shaped the individuals and the family. For instance, the loss of parents, extreme poverty, malnutrition, child abuse, poor school attendance or performance, adoption, psychiatric illnesses, and criminal records may all be a part of the factual dimension (Boszormenyi-Nagy & Krasner, 1986). Predetermined or irreversible facts will have a dynamic effect on individual development. Therefore, the facts of the family through various stages of the life cycle must be traced. A good method of tracing these developmental facts is to create a family genogram (McGoldrick & Gerson, 1985). Genograms allow the therapist to organize important factual information by creating a family tree in the first few sessions. Besides being a good assessment tool, genograms can be used in the intervention process. They also serve as a joining technique with all family members.

Assessment of Individual Psychology

The individual psychology dimension is a subjective realm that involves learning, conditioning, behavior, and development. It is difficult for any one psychological theory to account for all these different modalities, but it is necessary for the therapist to gain some appreciation and insight into the personality and development of each individual in the family. Here, it is important not to classify individuals into diagnostic categories that may overemphasize behavioral tendencies (Boszormenyi-Nagy & Krasner, 1986). The essential assessment area of individual psychology for the therapist is to learn how responsible individuals in the family are and what interventions will work best with the family.

Responsibility through individuation and differentiation is essential to understanding individuals in the contextual framework. As an individual becomes aware of his or her identity and constructs boundaries that differentiate from others, the person is able to become responsible in fair consideration of others (Boszormenyi-Nagy & Krasner, 1986). In other words, as people gain identity apart from others, they move to interact to get their own needs met. They move to reciprocal interactions in relationships because they know that the way to get fair consideration for their needs in relationships is to give fair consideration to others. This assessment of the individual psychology of each family member in terms of individuation and responsibility is essential for the therapist to understand the family members' potential in giving to one another in a reciprocal fashion.

It is important for the therapist to understand some of the developmental issues that have contributed to each family member's psyche. As we have mentioned before, these will often become evident during the life-validation and life-review stages of therapy and are understood best in terms of Erikson's psychosocial development. Erikson, Erikson, and Kivnick (1986) have illustrated how each psychosocial crisis has various potentials for the psychic development of individuals. An adapted form of this illustration is

Maladaptive Tendency	Psychosocial Crisis	Malignant Tendency	Adaptive Strength
Sensory maladjustment	Trust vs. mistrust	Withdrawal	Hope
Shameless willfulness	Autonomy vs. shame/doubt	Compulsion	Will
Ruthlessness	Initiative vs. guilt	Inhibition	Purpose
Narrow virtuosity	Industry vs. inferiority	Inertia	Competence
Fanaticism	Identity vs. role confusion	Repudiation	Fidelity
Promiscuity	Intimacy vs. isolation	Exclusivity	Love
Overextension	Generativity vs. stagnation	Rejectivity	Care
Presumption	Integrity vs. despair	Disdain	Wisdom

Figure 4.1.   Adaptive Tendencies of Psychosocial Development

found in Figure 4.1. Adaptive strengths are present in the individual if he or she negotiates the psychosocial crisis in realistic balance. Maladaptive tendencies are found in individuals who were imbalanced at one end of the psychosocial crisis—for instance, were too trusting or too autonomous. The malignant tendencies are found in individuals who were unable to negotiate the crisis. This framework is important to assessment because it enables the therapist to credit each family member's individual position and perspective in the relational reality. It also gives the therapist crucial insight into what issues will be most important to each family member, thereby making the therapist more of an advocate for each person in therapy.

Assessment of Family or Systemic Transactions

In assessing the family or systemic interactions, it is essential for the therapist to understand the communication process and power alignments in the family. These communication patterns and power hierarchies give key information on how to go about intervening with the family in order to change behavioral patterns that serve as barriers to balancing the intergenerational ledger.

The first area of this dimension encompasses the family members' involvement with one another. In other words, is the family *disengaged* or *enmeshed* (Minuchin, 1974). Stierlin (1973) describes similar family involvement as *centripetal* or *centrifugal*. In disengaged families, the members generally are uninvolved with each other. There may be a general lack of caring between them, making it very difficult to get them to interact with one another. Family members are not connected in terms of each other's thoughts and emotional processes. As mentioned earlier, many aging families have several disengaged characteristics simply because their members live in different localities and have little weekly contact.

In enmeshed families the members are generally overly involved with one another. There is usually a disregard for individual or personal boundaries that reduces any given member's self-identity. One family member will think, speak, and act on another's behalf. Self-delineation in these families may be so vague that problems for one family member may cause unbearable pain for another. Whereas it is difficult to get disengaged families to interact, enmeshed families make validation difficult, because individual responsibility becomes lost in a global emotional field of members feeling and acting on each other's behalf.

The second concern in assessing this dimension concerns the family communication. Communication, whether verbal or nonverbal, specifies family meanings and rules. Important to well-functioning families is the clarity of communication matching meta-communication (Bateson, 1972) or verbal matching nonverbal. If communication is unclear, there is a high potential for double-bind messages (Bateson, Jackson, Haley, & Weakland, 1956). For instance, an older mother may insist that her daughters show love for her, but then berate them because they do not let her be independent. When the daughters in turn distance themselves to let the mother be independent, they are accused of not caring. Such messages hinder responsible family interactions. Another communication concern is the level of honesty in the family. The members of some families may be hesitant to talk honestly with one another and will avoid painful or emotionally charged subjects. In these families, members sometimes will talk about other members when they are not present, make important family decisions alone, and actively deceive one another.

A final concern in assessing this dimension involves the power hierarchy and alignments in the family. In order to intervene and learn from families in a constructive manner, the power structure of the family must be gleaned. Many times the base of power will be made overt in the communication patterns of the family. For instance, one person is responsible for the group communication. A person in this position may speak for others, may tell them how to interpret others' communications, and may monitor others' communications. Such a person would be extremely powerful. Generally, power can be understood in terms of which persons make things happen in the family or prevent things from happening in the family. Very often, this power is vested in a coalition. Although spousal and parental coalitions are common, it is also very normal to find intergenerational coalitions of parent/child or grandparent/grandchild. These coalitions are usually formed against another member or generation. For instance, a grandmother and granddaughter may have a power coalition against the mother. When the mother tries to parent her daughter, the grandmother may step in as an "authority" or as the mother's mother and neutralize the authority by suggesting another style of parenting or informing the granddaughter that she does not have to obey the mother's rules.

It is important to realize that as with any family, but especially with an intergenerational aging family, the family system is not the only system that operates. Complex community and social systems become more important as an aging family requires additional resources. Boundaries and communications among neighbors, friends, social services, medical services, and support agencies become so intermixed at times that expectations become unclear (Wolinsky, 1990).

Assessment of Relational Ethics

The assessment of the fourth dimension of relational ethics is the most important component in the relational reality of the family. The intergenerational processes of fairness, reliability, and trustworthiness are key to this dimension (Boszormenyi-Nagy & Krasner, 1986). An initial step in assessing this dimension is to determine equity in the balance between what an individual is obligated to give to the family and what the individual is entitled to receive. This equity is ferreted out in dialogue with the family and is evident as members talk about fairness, being cheated, being underbenefited or overbenefited. For instance, if a person feels that his or her life has been characterized by giving too much without benefiting, the emotional field will usually include anger. This may take the form of open manipulation with loud and constant bickering and complaining, or the anger may be more subtle and take the form of passive-aggressive behavior. Sibling issues of unfairness are part of the conflicts that may surface. This can be seen in the example of a daughter who felt she was entitled to more of her mother's care and concern but saw that the mother was primarily involved with her son, the daughter's brother.

> "I quit. I am the one who has cared for Mother all these years and always been here when she needed anything. But I never hear anything like 'thanks' or 'I'm so proud of you.' All I get is how my brother is 'marvelous' and 'great' and he doesn't do one thing to help. He just comes in once a month and stays for an hour and Mother tells everyone how 'wonderful' a son she has. I'm here everyday. All I get is complaints and I'm sick of it. If she thinks he's so wonderful, he can take care of her."

People who have given too much without receiving their just entitlement feel that they have been cheated out of their fair share. They may then become cynical to the point that they are unable to recognize efforts of other family members to give to them. They may discount the efforts of others as being too meager and tend to depend on their own self-sufficiency. However, they do still hold family members responsible for fulfilling entitlement needs. This puts the family in an awkward position in which the individual refuses to take what the family offers, but holds the family accountable for its inability or unwillingness to give enough. Such situations portray a severe deterioration of trust in the family.

On the other hand, family members who consistently over-benefit from the family and do not fulfill obligations may experience guilt. People in this position may feel fearful and helpless, having taken so much from the family that they feel overwhelmed by a sense of indebtedness. Having been cared for all their lives without giving care in return, they may not see any other option but to continue the pattern. Generally, these people lack a clear sense of identity and self-esteem; they are irresponsible in fulfilling their familial roles. Such is the case with this 73-year-old woman who had constant anxiety about being alone.

"I am constantly terrified that something will happen to my husband or my children. I have always had them with me and I just don't know what I would do if they were gone. Who would take care of me? I've always needed someone with me who would look out after me. I guess, if my husband dies, I will have to depend more on the goodness of my daughter."

This statement was made in the presence of the daughter and was a clear effort by the mother to manipulate the daughter into comforting her by offering to continue to care for her if the father died. Such action indicates that the mother does not take responsibility for herself and even sees herself as incapable of caring for herself. Besides the symptomatology that the anxiety creates, trust-worthiness is depleted in the intergenerational system.

As we have seen in the previous chapter, imbalances in the

intergenerational family ledger often are due to injustices perpetrated in the previous generation. For instance, an older mother
who sacrificed enormously during her young and middle adult
years to take care of her sickly husband may feel she is entitled
to care from her son. However, the son may feel that he was denied
proper care and nurturing because the mother was too involved
with the father's illness. Thus he may refuse to care for his mother
as she ages. This is an example of how injustices and imbalances
are carried over from one generation to the next. When violations
are severe, individuals will often use destructive means of securing
their entitlement. These will vary, depending on the violation; they
can range from rewriting wills so adult children are excluded from
inheritance to emotional cutoffs to suicide attempts.

Loyalty is another important construct in the relational ethics
dimension. It is the obligative concern and care the individual gives
to the family. Loyalty to family, because it is an obligation, can often
be a weapon when members deny their loyalty to one another or
use it as a manipulative device. For instance, an elderly father may
tell his only daughter that she is uncaring because she spends more
time looking after her nuclear family than she does him. He may
openly manipulate her on this basis, and the daughter may feel
torn about where to spend her time. In this situation, two individuals stake a claim on the daughter in terms of obligations—her
husband and her father. Because the demands of one means sac-
rificing the other, the daughter is in a situation of *split loyalty*
(Boszormenyi-Nagy & Krasner, 1986). Such split loyalties are common in intergenerational aging families and can be the root of
tremendous relational deterioration.

Assessing the relational ethics dimension is complex and difficult because of the many relationships, both vertical and horizontal, that exist in the family. The Relational Ethics Scale
(Hargrave, Jennings, & Anderson, 1991) is a self-report instrument
that was developed to assist in the assessment of this fourth dimension. The 24-item questionnaire measures the constructs of trust
and justice, entitlement, and loyalty in both vertical and horizontal

relationships. Although this instrument is an asset to the therapist, it is no substitute for the therapist's exploration into individual and family concerns of justice, trust, entitlement, loyalty, responsibility, and reciprocity.

In working with aging families, this emotional field in the relational ethics dimension is the most essential object of therapy. If there is a rejunctive effort to balance justice in the family by fair giving and taking, trustworthiness is established and the family and older person can actively work on finishing well. If the emotional field is not addressed effectively, then the family continues harboring the same imbalances which results in little modification of dysfunctional actions.

CONCLUSION

Aging families have a complex task of negotiating difficult losses and making reconciliation with the past. Using the contextual framework, the therapist uses the techniques of life validation, life review, and intervention in a three-stage therapeutic process to deal with these relational issues. Using the four dimensions of relational reality from contextual therapy, the therapist organizes his or her assessment of individual and family concerns.

It is easy to get bogged down in the task of helping older families. Physical and health barriers may be many. Cognitive impairment may pose significant difficulty. The tasks of securing sufficient care and supervision may be enormous. It is easy for the emotional and relational concerns of the intergenerational ledger to be crowded out by simple lack of time. But the relational ethics dimension is the key to securing long-range family security and trust. The therapist must work to build this trust in the beginning stages of therapy.

5

LIFE VALIDATION

Anyone who has ever been a victim of a burglary will tell you how much he or she felt violated. First, a stranger gains access to a home through some means of illegal entry and then rummages carelessly through personal items and treasures in search for something valuable. To enter your own home and realize that you have been a "victim" can be devastating. Further, it is humiliating on some level to have someone who has no regard for you go through your belongings and steal those things deemed of value.

As therapists, we need to be careful not to barge into older people's lives uninvited. Older people, no matter how they have lived their lives, have years of treasures—many of which are only important to them. These treasures are found in their individual perspectives of history as they have lived, loved, fought, and struggled through the years. Even when we intend to be helpful, as therapists we often make the mistake of searching for only "valuable" therapeutic information. Then we use this information as we will in "helping" the family. Therapy with the aging family and the older person is different. We must be invited by the older person to examine his or her valuable story through dialogue. Then we must hold these very personal items carefully and ask thoughtful questions until we understand a little of what it means to the older person. Without this sensitivity, we may be perceived as burglars stealing the person's and aging family's history.

This initial process of joining with the aging family, and particularly with the older person, is called life validation. It is a therapeutic technique that the therapist can use in the initial sessions to join with the people in therapy, to build dialogue, and set the stage for a trustworthy therapeutic exchange. Although this technique can be done with the entire family present, it is most often carried out with just the eldest members of the family. Initial dialogues between the therapist and the older person join them in an intergenerational quest for understanding the legacies and ledgers of the past.

THEORETICAL BACKGROUND AND BASICS OF THE TECHNIQUE

Life validation (Asnes, 1983) grows out of the approach of life review (Butler, 1963) and psychosocial development (Erikson, 1963). The approach is intended to give the therapist important information about significant developmental periods in the older client's life. The main thrust of the technique is for the therapist to use his or her general knowledge of macrohistorical events to stimulate conversation with the older person concerning his or her microhistorical perspective on these events. In other words, the older person usually has decades of experience of which the therapist has no firsthand knowledge. However, if the therapist is aware of the major world and national events of those decades, there is a forum for initiating dialogue about the person's life at that time.

In choosing the historical events to use in the life-validation process, the therapist should try to refer to periods that are easy to recall and are at different individual and family developmental stages. For instance, for a cohort of 80-year-old people, the therapist might choose to use the following six historical events.

World War I

In the late teens, the 80-year-old cohort would have been of school age. Although the United States entered World War I later in the conflict, it was a time of great patriotism. Families sacrificed for the cause and there was a clarity of purpose for fighting the war. Before the war, the United States was made up of a primarily agricultural population and it was a fairly new international power. After World War I, the United States was the most powerful nation in the world and the population shifted so that the majority of people lived in the cities. Many older people had fathers or brothers who served during the conflict.

One can see how the war environment would have affected a child negotiating the tasks of *initiative versus guilt* and *industry versus inferiority*. Society would have expected much in terms of patriotism and compliance and thus gaining a sense of competence would have demanded that children adhere to strict expectations. Some older people look back on this conflict as a source of pride in their country when everyone contributed to a common good. The following is from an interview with a 79-year-old woman recounting the war effort.

"Everybody seemed together then. We planted these victory gardens in the front yard so everyone in the neighborhood could see. Sometimes it would be a real competition as to who had the best garden."

"So everyone did their part for the cause of democracy," responded the therapist.

The woman added, "I remember my father taking all of the family to a war bond rally. There was a band playing and flags waving and several speakers. I don't remember what they said, but at the end of the rally my father gave each child enough money to purchase a bond. We were all so proud. I swear, the way the children felt that day you would have thought we personally had won the war."

But the war experience was not a pleasant one for everyone. Imagine how this 78-year-old woman, whose brother was killed in the conflict when she was a young girl, would have felt about the united war effort or a war bond rally.

"How did the family respond after the news about your brother?" asked the therapist.

"We were sad. Things just didn't get back to normal. Thomas was the only boy in the family and Daddy planned to have him live on the farm and pass it along to him. My family eventually sold the land—our home place. We missed him and I don't think Daddy ever really got over it."

Ratification of 19th Amendment, Spanish Influenza Epidemic

The decade of the 1920s was a time of tremendous change in the life-styles of Americans. Riding on a crest of power and prosperity, new individual and family freedoms were explored. The adoption of the 19th amendment giving women the right to vote was only part of the shift in roles for women. This was the age of the flapper, when women cut their hair, threw off their corsets, shortened their dresses, and began to make decisions for themselves. This was the first wave of the women's movement and it was an exciting time for both women and men.

A cohort of 80-year-old people would be in their adolescence during the 1920s. One can imagine that the emphasis on personal freedom and change that came with the period would have a dynamic effect on individuals facing the psychosocial crisis of *identity versus role confusion*. The 1920s have often been likened to the 1960s in terms of the younger generation's challenging as a group the societal expectations and mores of the older generation. Some therapists who experienced the 1960s actually have much in common with these 80-year-old flappers who lived through the 1920s.

In the late teens and early '20s, a Spanish influenza epidemic claimed thousands of lives and many people lost part of their families. As is still the case, the very young and the old were the ones who were the most vulnerable to influenza. For many older people, then in their early teens, this was their first experience with death, and it had a profound impact on their family. This was the case of a 76-year-old woman who was the eldest of five children.

Woman: I was born in March, the following year my sister was born in May, and the following year my brother was born in June. Then came the two girls, who died within six months of one another. Allie was a little over three years old and the baby was really a baby. They both died in the epidemic.

Therapist: Didn't you say before that Allie was the apple of your father's eye?

Woman: Yes. Oh, he suffered terribly from that loss, but it also made him very tender to the rest of the children. He didn't ever want us to catch him crying because he thought that we would think that we had done something wrong.

One of the characteristics of this woman was that she kept emotions very much to herself. Here is an example from her past of how her parents taught her how to handle the grief of loss. The father did not want the children to assume that they had done something to cause grief, so he sealed off his grief even though the family knew he was in pain. This and other incidents in the woman's life probably taught her how to maintain positions of emotional distance.

The Great Depression

Without a doubt, the Great Depression is the historical event of the 20th century that has shaped the older cohort's development as a group more than any other event. During this time of overwhelming unemployment and despair, families made enormous sacrifices in order to ensure survival. Starvation or deprivation was a realistic possibility for a large percentage of the population, and panic and anxiety were common.

The 80-year-old at this time would have been entering his or her young adulthood years and dealing with the psychosocial crisis of *intimacy versus isolation*. At exactly the time that many of these older people were trying to form intimate bonds with a spouse, basic survival was being challenged. If we think back to Maslow's (1970) hierarchy of needs, we can understand that it is difficult for an individual to deal with the quest for intimacy or belonging when basic physiological or safety needs are in question. Most older people were affected in some way by the Great Depression— some were affected profoundly. Many delayed marriage or did not marry at all. Some were forced to move to different geographic locations in search of work. Those family members who had work felt the responsibility to care for other family members who were less fortunate; this was the case of this 86-year-old woman who had three daughters.

Woman: All the banks were closing around 1932 and it was terribly frightening.
Therapist: I've read a lot about the depression, but I don't know what it was like from a personal side. Did you or your husband have a job?
Woman: My husband was lucky to have had a job ever since we've been married.
Therapist: So your family was okay?
Woman: We were all right. My sister and her husband needed help so we gave them a place to live and helped them get back on their feet until he was able to get a job. The rest of the family wasn't able to help them—we were lucky to have jobs so we took care of them.

It is also important to remember that many of the people who make up the second generation of the family, or the adult children of the older people, were born during the decade of the 1930s. Thus when people of this generation were negotiating crucial initial stages of development in trust and autonomy, they were witness to the turmoil and problems of the period. This no doubt has had an effect on how this generation perceives family and how it now views its responsibility in the intergenerational family group.

World War II

World War II was the most consuming human catastrophe of our century. Millions of people worldwide lost their lives in the war, including more than 230,000 Americans. An unbelievable amount of monetary, material, and human resources were consumed in the biggest global conflict in history. There is little doubt that almost every person was touched by the war in some way. Although some older people or their spouses served in this conflict, most worked to supply and support the war effort. Also, some of the adult sons and daughters of these older people served in the military during the conflict.

Generativity versus stagnation would have been the psychosocial crisis that these older people, then in middle adulthood, would have been facing during the war. Uncertainty concerning how to care for the next generation or even to provide for their survival had to have been a central theme as control over the future was tenuous because of draft notices, military transfers, and communication blackouts. Again, individual sacrifice was great, but now it was instigated by worldwide enemies. Many older people lost loved ones in the war. This 71-year-old woman's husband and brother were killed in France.

Woman: When the war started, my husband was drafted and was killed. We knew that was it then. It was hard to give him up. But there was nothing we could do about it.
Therapist: What did you do after your husband was killed?
Woman: I had moved back with my mother when my husband

was drafted. I stayed with her. I kept my younger brothers
and sisters and my children while she worked.

Therapist: So you raised your children along with the rest of your
mother's children.

Woman: I did. I raised them until they were grown. One brother
was also killed in Europe during the war, so I lost a husband
and a brother.

In this woman's life, intimacy and care were both interrupted
by the war. Her efforts to achieve these goals were vandalized by
the deaths of a husband and a brother. Having been devastated
by prior losses, it was not surprising that this woman had a history
of being slightly overfocused on the care and nurturing of her own
and other people's children.

Korean Conflict and Cold War

The Korean conflict is a much overlooked war in our history in
terms of human costs. Almost 53,000 Americans died in this two-
year conflict, almost as many as in the entire Vietnam war.
Although there was not the all-out national focus on this conflict
as there was in World War II, families were affected a great deal.
Also, the 1950s were a time of world uneasiness as the cold war
between the United States and the Soviet Union escalated. Never
before was the threat of global holocaust through nuclear capability
such a real possibility. Along with the abundance and prosperity
of the 1950s were the paranoid fears of communist infiltration and
the fanaticism of McCarthyism.

The older cohort was still in the psychosocial crisis of
generativity versus stagnation. Older people who had children who
fought in the conflict faced the uncertainty of war and its effects
on their families. Most of these people became grandparents during the 1950s and they saw the now-adult children have children
of their own. In addition, many of the older people in this cohort
would have had their own parents die during this decade, thereby

becoming the eldest generation of the family with a special obligation to perpetuating the family. Again, the focus of the developmental stage was caring for the two younger generations in a potentially dangerous global atmosphere.

Assassination of John F. Kennedy

The assassination of the president triggers a very specific time and place memory for most older people. Even older people who have a significant level of dementia will often recall accurate details about the time when Kennedy was killed. Consider the case of this woman in her late 60s who lived in Fort Worth in 1963.

> "I remember there was a parade in Fort Worth the day that he [Kennedy] was killed before he went over to Dallas. We all lined up on the streets five or six deep. Everyone was waving and Jackie had on a beautiful pink dress. The woman next to me held up a big sign that said 'WE LOVE YOU JACK AND JACKIE.'
>
> "I went to work after lunch, and when I heard that he was shot—I just couldn't believe it. I had just seen him that morning."

This woman, who had difficulty recalling information, was able to give an authoritative, first-person account of actually having seen Kennedy on the day he was killed. She was truly an expert on that day. It is clear that recalling this information would raise her self-esteem, assuming that the therapist were thoughtful enough to ask.

The 1960s were a time of great turmoil in our nation's history with the civil rights movement, the war in Vietnam, and the anti-war movement. Old values were openly questioned. It also was a time of fruition for technological advancement. One 82-year-old woman, in recalling men landing on the moon, commented that she had traveled to Oklahoma as a girl in a wagon and, in 1969, had seen men walking on the moon. This older cohort has indeed seen phenomenal changes.

Most of the older 80-year-old cohort would have been approaching their retirement years in the 1960s. Refocusing on their spousal relationships and dealing with the reality of their accomplishments at work and at home, these individuals would have been ready to enter the last psychosocial crisis of *integrity versus despair.* This generation had to begin focusing on past life accomplishments at a time of massive change—when the value of the past itself was being questioned.

THERAPEUTIC USES OF VALIDATION

Validation means that the therapist affirms the older person's sense of accomplishment and history, which is, of course, the concept of partiality in contextual therapy. As the older person's life position, story, and contribution are acknowledged by the therapist, three therapeutic goals are accomplished. The first goal that is addressed is that the older person's self-esteem is raised. Older people, who encounter numerous physical difficulties such as loss of sight, hearing, and mobility, are faced daily with problems of functioning in the environment. When this is combined with short-term memory difficulties and cognitive slowness, a hurried society that focuses on the future would certainly challenge the older person's competence. As competence is challenged, self-esteem erodes. Therefore, it is essential for the therapist to provide the opportunity to build the self-esteem of the older person.

The older person is the expert on his or her own history. As the therapist opens up the dialogue with a discussion of the historical period, numerous occasions arise to affirm the older person. As Asnes (1983) reports, many unarticulate and depressed older people become animated and involved once the validation process has begun. The key to raising the self-esteem of the older person using this technique is always to let the older person be the expert and affirm his or her life and ability in whatever way possible. For instance, in the following example, an 86-year-old woman was quite concerned about her memory difficulty.

Woman: I've always had, what you call a photogenic memory. I could always remember things that other people would forget. But lately it is slipping. I can remember old things, but the things that have happened in the last few days give me trouble.

Therapist: So you can remember as clear as a bell the things that happened a long time ago, but the you need a little help in remembering things that happened recently.

Woman: That's right. I can remember once a person says something. I'll be 87 years old in June, and I still have most of my senses.

Therapist: That's for sure. I don't know too many 87-year-old people who have a photogenic memory.

Woman: I have always remembered well. For instance, I can remember all sorts of geography I learned in the sixth grade. Like there is a point in southern Africa where you can see three oceans—the Indian, Antarctic, and Atlantic.

This woman, faced with the difficulty of living with a loss of short-term memory, is concerned that her mind is slipping. The therapist validates the woman by normalizing the memory loss by commenting that if she gets simple verbal cues, she is able to remember. He further validates her photographic memory by commenting on her photogenic mind, being careful to use the same incorrect terminology. In the validation process, the therapist should do nothing to impinge on the older person's expert position. This comment raises the self-esteem of the woman as she recounts her sixth-grade geography. As she remembers, she now validates herself.

In another example, a woman in her 70s, who had no known living relative, was placed in the personal care facility by a court-appointed guardian. The woman had substantial dementia and was disoriented about time and place. She was fiercely independent and was confused and angry about being placed in the home. The woman had a severely disfigured right arm.

Therapist: Tell me about your arm.

Woman: I was three years old. My mother was showing her brothers how to paint the house. She went into the house and I went up the ladder. When she came out, I went down. (holding her arm in the air with a smile) This is the result. My mother took me to town where the doctor operated here, here, here, and here. (pointing to several scars)

Therapist: It must have been quite a fall.

Woman: It's never stopped me. I can write with both hands. Give me a pencil and paper and I'll prove it to you.

At this point, the therapist validated the woman by letting her show him that she could indeed write with both hands. Her self-esteem and confidence were raised and this once-angry and uncooperative woman now was comfortable in informing the therapist about some of her past. Later in the session, she revealed that she never knew her father and that her mother died when the woman was 12. She was raised by her grandmother until her grandmother died when the woman was 18. The woman survived and had a successful career mending hosiery despite being alone and handicapped. It was very easy for the therapist to validate this woman's fierce independence and sense of accomplishment.

Although this woman was validated during the session, her dementia was such that accessing other past events was very difficult. She spoke vaguely of an old neighborhood in the city. The therapist, during one session, took the woman to a place where he thought the neighborhood might be. Before long, the woman became animated as she began to recognize landmarks. She then began to direct the therapist. Within minutes, the woman had located her grandmother's house, which she had not seen in 50 years, and the elementary school that she had attended. Although still she was severely limited, the trip validated the woman and it helped her to access new areas of memory. One can only imagine the pride and self-esteem the woman felt as she came back from the trip and told one of the personal care aides, "I went home today."

The second goal of the technique of life validation is for the therapist to gain initial information concerning the family and individual development issues. Although the gathering of this information will not provide enough specifics to gain thorough details of individual psychology or relational ethics dimensions, it does begin to give the therapist a rough sketch of salient therapeutic issues that can be followed up later in the life-review process. In the following example, an older widow's periodic bouts with depression and confusion centered on feelings of being deserted and not being needed by her family. When asked about the Great Depression, this 71-year-old woman recounted her personal sacrifice to her family of origin in caring for her sickly father and her mother's younger children.

Mother: We stayed where we were—we had a little farm. My father died in the spring. He died of—well, it was too high an altitude for the shape he was in. We didn't know what in the world would happen to us. I think I was about 13 or 14. I was the one who stayed up with my father every night about a month before he died. I'd keep a wet cloth on his face, fan him, and give him his medicine.

Therapist: You said it was harder to lose your father than it was your mother.

Woman: It was. I guess I felt I was the only one who could take

care of him. He use to call me his little nurse. Mother didn't
need that kind of attention. Of course, she had so many little
ones to take care of. She gave all of us a job to do. Certain
ones would take care of children, some would feed chickens,
milk the cows—whatever needed to be done, each one had
a job. But mother was a wonderful woman that she could
go on and take care of 12 children.

Therapist: She stepped right in. Did she go to work at a job that
paid?

Woman: She did. She took a job at the laundry and left me there
to raise the children. I did okay—especially with the little
ones. I have always felt that was my special job—to take care
of the little ones.

This woman had a preoccupation with caring for babies.
Her family confirmed that she was an excellent caretaker of
babies and was very nurturing. But now that her age and
physical problems prevented her from taking care of the family,
she felt she was displaced from her role—a role that she
learned from an earlier period was essential to family survival.
Besides validating the woman's sacrifice and role in the family,
this information greatly clarified the ledger issues from the
older woman's perspective.

The third goal of the life-validation technique is to build
trust between the older person and the therapist. This trust is
essential to the therapeutic process for two reasons. As the
elder in the family, the older person has tremendous resources
to empower the aging family. Dysfunctional patterns, unfinished
business, beliefs, interactional patterns, and traditions can all be
changed or transferred to the family. When the therapist joins
with the older person, he or she can become a dual advocate
for the intergenerational family. If the therapist and older person do not establish trust, they will tend to neutralize each
other's effect in the family. Further, the relationship between the

therapist and the older person serves as a model of trustworthy dialogue to the rest of the family.

In the following example, notice how the widowed older woman trusts the therapist in teaching him about her cultural heritage. Each time the therapist validates the woman's Croation background, she is willing to specify a little more about her life. This level of trust is a substantial improvement, especially considering the fact that the woman is angry at her caretaking daughter and feels that the daughter is trying to take away her independence. The woman, just prior to the session, had refused meals and medications because "she could take care of herself and did not need anyone's help."

Therapist: Your father applied for citizenship as soon as he got off the boat?

Woman: As soon as he got the opportunity to. He was a very fine house painter. He could even do murals. He was artistic and would do the sketching and painting himself.

Therapist: So he not only painted, houses, he was a mural artist. He must have been a very talented man.

Woman: Oh yes. He also had a very fine tenor voice.

Therapist: Really?

Woman: Really. And not only that, he spoke four languages. He spoke Italian. He spoke Polish. He spoke Croation. He spoke English. And my mother was from a Slavic neighborhood also. They met in Philadelphia and were married. My mother was a very fine seamstress. She was so skilled at making wardrobes and was sought after.

Therapist: And so what was their name—your maiden name?

Woman: My name is Annisa Pavisa Sonilich. Pavisa is Croation for Paulina and Annisa was my godmother's name. When I met my husband and his name was so simple, I think I would have just married him for the name.

Therapist: Now tell me your name again—how you pronounce it.

Woman: It's not so bad, you just sound it out. S, O, N, sone, I, a L, I, C, H, lich. Sonilich. Annisa Pavisa Sonilich.

Therapist: Annisa Pavisa Sonilich.

Woman: That's right. You got it. This was also my mother's name. The eldest daughter is always named after the mother.

Therapist: Did your father and mother teach you to speak Croation?

Woman: Oh yes. We wouldn't have understood half of what was said if we didn't speak Croation. It was spoken in the home, but we had to learn English.

Therapist: Well, you have very fine English for someone coming from a European background.

Woman: Well, darlin', that's because the translation of English is the more proper than what is spoken. It's no credit to me personally, other than the fact that I'm European and that's how all European children are taught.

CONCLUSION

The beginning stage of therapy often determines how the therapy will end. Using the contextual therapy approach, the initial dialogue between the therapist and the family is essential in the trust-building effort. The trust reserves are desperately needed later in therapy when intergenerational ledger imbalances have to be addressed directly. With the aging family, the life-validation technique provides that therapist with an organized context in which to pursue this important dialogue. Life validation enhances the client's self-esteem, reveals important developmental themes, and builds trust.

It has also been our experience that the validation process builds into the life of the therapist. Helping professionals are often affected by our ageist society. For many therapists, the life-validation approach gives them their first opportunity to really experience the contribution and lives of these older people. Our experience tells us that validation not only is an effective therapeutic technique that helps aging families, but is also a skill that helps therapists become better people, harboring fewer prejudices against the older population.

6

LIFE REVIEW

When someone has seen a great movie or read a great book, he or she often wants to read the book or see the movie again. People tend to organize their own opinions and thoughts around books or movies, and they usually enjoy discussing certain points of the work. These discussions seldom focus on the entire work, but rather concentrate on specific elements that were important to the story or that held particular meaning for the viewer. This type of conversation often enhances the enjoyment and understanding of a given work.

Older people and aging families also want to "read over" or "see" parts of their lives again. In looking back, turning points or dynamic events can be identified as sculptors of the family relationships and life. Talking about these issues can help a person clarify and organize his or her thinking about life, thereby enriching the meaning of his or her own life story. Just as various forms of punctuation help to clarify a manuscript, specific events punctuate people's lives, giving meaning and organization to them throughout the life course. The process of "looking back" is called life review (Butler, 1963).

In Chapter 4, we referred to life review as the second stage in doing contextual family therapy with aging families. This chapter explains the basic idea of the life-review process; then the role of life review in doing contextual family therapy with aging families is considered. The chapter concludes with clinical examples that illustrate this second stage of therapy.

THEORETICAL BACKGROUND OF LIFE REVIEW

If we look at the life cycle from birth to old age and then death, we see that normal life stages of growth and development are apparent. The first year of life has its own tasks and growth points, as do adolescence and middle age. This same line of thinking applies to the last stage of life and that of aging family members (see Chapter 1). As we have already noted, the final stage involves a gradual shift of family power to the younger generations. The middle generation provides more care and nurturing, whereas the older generation focuses more on support for adult children and on sharing the wisdom acquired over many years of life. A final task of the family is the preparation for the death of the oldest members.

Butler (1963) has conceptualized "life review as a naturally occurring, universal mental process, characterized by the progressive return to consciousness of past experiences, and, particularly, the resurgence of unresolved conflicts; simultaneously, and normally, these revived experiences and conflicts can be surveyed and reintegrated" (p. 66). Thus life review is seen as a natural response to approaching death. This same life-review process often occurs in much younger persons who are facing death: soldiers before battle, the fatally ill, or those condemned to die. When famous aging persons publish their memoirs, they are in some way sharing with us their life-review process.

Erik Erikson (1963) observed that "identity formation neither begins with nor ends with adolescence; it is a lifelong development largely unconscious to the individual and to his society" (p. 113). Adolescents are in the midst of explosive personal growth: physical, emotional, psychological, and interpersonal. Butler (1963) notes that adolescents "frequently spend time examining themselves in mirrors" (p. 75). As they look at themselves, they ask, "Who am I?" At the other end of the life cycle, the elderly are facing clear declines in cognitive, perceptual, and psychomotor functions. In a somewhat similar vein, the elderly look into the mirror of their personal life reviews and ask themselves, "Who was I? Who have I become?"

The thrust toward self-awareness, begun in infancy and intensified in adolescence, may well be at its peak in old age, due to the many experiences of a long life and increased personal time for reflection and review. As a result, many older persons manifest a deep personal integration and an ever-increasing wisdom, viewed by Minuchin and Fishman (1981) as "the knowledge of the interconnectedness of things" (p. 290).

Among many of the elderly who have lived a reasonably functional life, the normal life-review process seems to promote a substantial reorganization of the personality (Butler, 1963). This process can help to explain the wise serenity so often seen in healthy elderly persons. They manifest such qualities as flexibility, resilience, and self-awareness. Such elderly persons and their families will probably not present themselves for family therapy. These families have the capacity to work out their conflicts and to complete their lives in much the same way that they have lived them—in an adequate, functional and satisfying manner.

LIFE REVIEW AND CONTEXTUAL THERAPY WITH AGING FAMILIES

In working with aging families, the therapist first uses life validation, usually alone with the older person, as a way of joining, understanding, and supporting the older client as he or she tells his or her life story, perhaps for the last time. The second stage in this therapy is the life-review process. This process will often involve other family members, who are able to add important details and different perspectives. During the life-review process, the therapist pursues two main purposes: to discover which transgenerational issues are still unresolved in the multigenerational family system and to credit each family member for entitlements and obligations in the family. The life-review process thus enables the therapist to hypothesize about possible family imbalances in the transgenerational ledger. This can lead the therapist to look for specific points of intervention that can enable the family to redress these imbalances.

In his work with the elderly, Butler (1963) has observed that many of the elderly who are prone to anxiety, despair, depression, or even suicide are those who have experienced a painful life-review. He saw at least three groups who found their life-review process that disturbing. First, there were those who always avoided the present and focused on the future. Now in their aging present, they see most of their life behind them, with a greatly reduced future ahead. As they come toward the end of their life, old age cannot deliver on those past hopes so rooted in the future.

Second, there are those people who have consciously and willfully exercised their potential to injure others. In their declining years, these people realize that many of those whom they have hurt are dead or are for some reason unavailable to them. These elderly persons must now deal with their guilt and the possibility that they may never have the chance to ask for or receive forgiveness from the people they have hurt. Finally, people who are arrogant and prideful—whose lives have centered around themselves— suddenly become keenly aware that the world will go on without them. What a blow to the ego! Worst of all, maybe their family will be relieved once they are dead!

In our attempts to help the family rebalance the intergenerational ledger, we have encountered deep, touching experiences of forgiveness, reconciliation, intimacy, and family union. Butler (1963) states that "in the course of the life review, the older person may reveal to his wife, children, and other intimates, unknown qualities of his character and unstated actions of his past; in return, they may reveal heretofore undisclosed or unknown truths. Hidden themes of great vintage may emerge, changing the quality of a lifelong relationship. Revelations of the past may forge a new intimacy, render a deceit honest; they may sever peculiar bonds and free tongues" (p. 75).

One such experience occurred to me, the second author, just a few months ago. My oldest brother, the first of nine children, was dying in a nursing home 1500 miles away. I decided to fly to his bedside while he was still alive, rather than wait for his death and then attend his funeral. About 25 years ago, my brother became responsible for the care of our ailing father, then a widower. My brother resented that some of our siblings did not share in the financial burden of paying for our father's nursing home stay. After our father died, my brother's wife soon passed away as well. Childless, my brother withdrew from regular contact with almost all of his siblings. It was such a shock, after so many years of being cut off, to see my brother in his dying state. During those three days at the nursing home, I reconnected with him in a powerful but painful way. When his mind drifted or he dozed off in fitful sleep, I sat at his bedside, read my Bible, and said prayers of thanksgiving for such a wonderful, caring brother. When his mind returned to my world, we shared many, many memories of our childhood during the Great Depression, of his life work in the military and the police force, and of our losses—our parents, his wife, a brother and a sister, and now his approaching death.

Those were three bittersweet days. Just about one hour before I had to leave for the airport, he struggled to free his right arm from under the bedsheets. Then, in a hoarse voice, he whispered, "Bill, hold my hand. You, your wife and I are all going on a long journey. But I am going first. And I am scared." We both shed long, hard brotherly tears.

As I took leave of my only remaining brother, I held his hand, kissed him, and whispered in his ear: "I love you and I will miss you." I left the room in tears, never to see him again. One week later, almost to the hour, he died. Butler was right; my brother and I had forged a new intimacy.

In doing life review with elderly clients, therapists may indeed profit from the following observations of Butler (1963). First, a personal sense and meaning of the life cycle are more clearly unfolded by those older people who are at the end of life. Some younger family therapists may wonder about the value of doing family therapy with those near death. However, this gift from the older client benefits not only the younger generations in the family, but also the younger family therapist who is still at a much earlier place in the life cycle. Wisdom is such a treasure!

Second, the elderly are best helped by a therapist who is a participant observer. This comment can readily apply to all levels of therapy, but it is especially helpful in working with older clients. They need and want a therapist who is able to listen (even to repeated stories!) to them and to tolerate and understand them. Third, the therapist needs to help the elderly to "integrate past life experiences as they have been lived, not as they might have been lived" (Butler, 1963). Family therapists who are attempting to do just that in their own lives probably have the best chance to help the elderly come to grips with their own unchangeable past and to deal with their real, rather than desired, personal history.

THE TECHNIQUE OF LIFE REVIEW

Older people and their families will most often center the life-review process on substantial or important events or conflicts in the family past. In order to gain the necessary information concerning the intergenerational ledger, it is important that the therapist be aware of certain aspects and techniques of the life-review process. A life review takes patience and understanding. The therapist must listen well and tolerate the repetition of stories. As we have mentioned before, the role of the therapist shifts to that of a commentator on family interaction and relationships as he or she gives more overt credit to each member's position in the family.

One of the more important aspects of the life review requires that the therapist help family members deal with the truth about the past. Unresolved conflicts and unfinished family business do not just go way because they are buried. These issues are buried alive and often come back to haunt the aging family. Although the therapist may be tempted to reframe these issues to put them in a more positive light, it is essential that the family members deal with the issues as they see them from their frame of reference. Reframing may help the family avoid the issue itself, but it will do nothing to correct the imbalance in the intergenerational ledger that the issue has caused. The therapist must help the family deal with the reality of the past and integrate it into the present reality. This task can be very uncomfortable for both the family and the therapist, and it takes a substantial amount of courage. In the following example, an eldest daughter and her parents face the tough issue that the mother has been an emotional burden on the rest of the family.

Therapist: (to the mother) Your depression throughout these years, how has it affected you?

Mother: It has put me in terrible pain. I am always worried that something terrible is going to happen to my family.

Therapist: How would you deal with the fear?

Mother: I would just go on. I would check up on the family.

Therapist: How do you think your depression and fear affected your family?

Mother: I don't think I was depressed that much. I don't think it affected them. They know I love them.

Therapist: Depression and fear are almost always a burden. (looking toward the daughter) How did this depression and fear affect the family?

Daughter: My brother just cut off. Daddy just doesn't rock the boat. I guess I don't either and I just try to take care the best I can.

Therapist: What happened when you rocked the boat?

Daughter: Mother would get really depressed or cry all the time.

It has been taxing through the years. It has always been like this—it's only worse now.

Mother: But I haven't been depressed that much.

Daughter: Not all the time, but a whole bunch.

Therapist: That usually cuts down on what a person can give to the family.

Mother: You know I love you, don't you?

Daughter: I know you love me. But down through the years, and even now, it has been difficult to feel your love. I know that my brother feels that way too.

Mother: I haven't shown you enough. But I do love you. What can I do to really show you?

The therapist's willingness to bring up issues of burden and emotional responsibility with the mother helps her face the reality that her depression has taken a toll on the family. In turn, the daughter is willing to face the issue and be honest about the past with her mother—perhaps for the first time in years. When the mother does not get the reassurance from the daughter she has probably received in the past, she begins to integrate the truth into her life. This in turn spurs her to ask about how she can redress the wrong.

In another example, a 74-year-old woman held herself responsible for the death of her sister. The sister, then three years old, was killed when she was struck by an out-of-control automobile. The woman, then five years old, was with her sister at the time. The therapist helped the woman deal with the reality of the truth by addressing the blame with her little sister. Although this incident was an accident, the therapist did not make the judgment. Instead, he gave the woman the opportunity to address the blame herself.

Therapist: So you were five and your sister was three. So this occurred 69 years ago.

Client: Yes. But it has colored every aspect of my life. It was a horrible event and I've always carried it with me.
Therapist: Your sister, would she blame you for her death?
Client: I don't think so. I don't know.
Therapist: Well you are 74. Close your eyes. Imagine that your sister—71 years old—is sitting with you here. (long pause) What will she say to you?
Client: (Starting to cry) It is not your fault. I have been happy and in a better place all these years. I love you and I know you love me. You need to go on with your life.

This woman was in terrible pain because of a childhood accident. Although she blamed herself for years, she reveals here her feelings that it was indeed an accident. The therapist helps the woman deal with the truth by letting her address the issue in an adult fashion with her adult little sister. This makes the reality of the accident come alive and allows the woman to integrate this incident into her current life. Instead of being responsible for a child's death, she faces the fact that they were both children and that, unfortunately, accidents occur. The woman was then freed to talk about the incident in terms of grief over lost opportunity without the cloud of blame.

A second important aspect of the life review is to pay particular attention to summary statements about relationships and life. Often these summary statements contain the essential elements of the overall character of one's life. For example, "I've lived a good life," or "If I had it to do over again, I wouldn't change a thing," indicate positive regard concerning the process of life review. One way to access these summary statements is to ask the older person or family to come up with an epitaph for a tombstone or with one sentence people would say about the older person after he or she died. A 71-year-old woman offered the following:

Therapist: What do you think they would put on your tombstone?
Client: Don't mess around with me.

Therapist: Interesting.

Client: I used to be a librarian and everybody knew they had to
   toe the line with me. I did not tolerate any misbehavior. I
   ran a tight ship and got the job done. I even had one school
   principal say that I ran the school from the library.

It is not surprising that this woman turned out to be an
extremely controlling woman with her family and in other relationships. Her summary statement serves notice that she is used
to having her way. It is also interesting to note that the epitaph
may also be a warning to the therapist in terms of a metaphor.
Summary statements often bring up vast amounts of despair, as
with the following older man.

Therapist: After you are gone, what do you think your family and
   friends will say about you?

Client: (tentatively) Probably that I was a no account. (long pause)
   I probably have not done much that people would respect
   me for.

This man revealed a great amount of pain when he summed
up his life. During the life review, he gave account after account
of how he abused friendships and family relationships and now
was left alone. Summary statements about life give the therapist
an overall report of the emotional condition in the
intergenerational ledger. He or she can then use these statements
to flesh out the specific information during the life review.

A third aspect of the life review to which the therapist needs
to pay particular attention concerns how past events and family
obligations now influence the present. Family members often fulfilled obligations toward their own aging parents years before and
they may expect these obligations to be compensated in turn by
their own children. For instance, a divorced woman who was
deserted by her husband may expect her children to show her great
devotion despite her mothering skills because she went to work

and provided for the family. Older people will often use tradition or past actions to define standards about aging. In the following example, an aging widow feels slighted by her son because he does not care for her in the way that she cared for her aging mother.

Client: Do all old people feel they're neglected?
Therapist: I know some who do and then I know some who don't.
Client: Well, I don't think my son and daughter-in-law give me much of their time.
Therapist: You feel neglected by them?
Client: Maybe it's old age working on me. Maybe it's because I took care of my mother at home until the day she died.

This woman felt neglected by her family because she anticipated they would fulfill the same obligation the way she had. Although the family made a clear effort to visit the mother daily, her standard of care required that she should live in one of the family member's homes. Certainly the family was not neglecting this woman, but the past events and obligations of the mother's life directly shaped her present belief that she was entitled to more care than she was receiving.

The life review process often reveals incongruent details about events or relationships. In other words, there are stories about the past or gaps in events that simply do not fit together. Often these gaps or incongruent stories indicate buried pain or unfinished family business. In the following example, a depressed older man with two adult children had divorced his wife after 20 years of marriage. He was asked by the therapist to bring some family photographs that represented the family at different stages. The man brought a few scattered photographs with large gaps between time periods.

Therapist: (Looking at the photographs) Do you and your family have many family reunions?
Client: As far as us having reunions, no, we don't have reunions.

As far as our immediate family, we don't get involved in reunions. We see each other regularly.

Therapist: How often do you get together as a family?

Client: Oh, about once a month.

Therapist: All of you get together?

Client: No, not all of us. We hardly ever all get together. They
have their lives. I don't get involved. We don't plan get togeth-
ers. If it happens, it happens.

The therapist continued with the client, asking about his own
family of origin, his marriage, his children, and his work. When
asked about his childhood, the client replied, "It was a likeable
home, but it was rough, as far as I can remember." When the therapist asked him about his marriage, he replied said, "We had some
good years. . . . But after I found out about the affairs, they weren't
so nice." The therapist then asked about what kind of support
he received during the divorce. The man answered, "I supported
myself. No help from anyone. I had my job. I lived on that."

When questioned about his jobs, the client recalled many details
of his adult work life and spoke in an animated way about his
work life and the satisfaction that it gave him. Then the therapist
moved to his memories of raising his two children as a single parent. At this point, his tone of voice became flat and he was vague
about details of his children's growing up. "The only thing I can
remember is that they grew up and got married. . . . I did the best
I could with what I had."

This older man had a clear memory when it came to recalling
his work career, but he was vague and evasive about the details
of the children's growing up. The lack of photographic record of
his children and his unenthusiastic attitude toward seeing them
indicated that there was emotional distance between this elderly
father and his adult children. Subsequent sessions with the client
and his adult children confirmed this clinical hypothesis.

There are many tools that can stimulate information during the
life review beyond the therapist and aging family simply talking.

Photographs provide an excellent way to access information about the past as does music representing certain time periods. Certain families identify their stories closely with books or movies. Often a family house or pieces of furniture will reflect the history of the family and give stimulus to more memories. One of the more creative life reviews we have witnessed was with an older widow who had several adult children. The woman was a wonderful cook and her family had been trying to get her to write down her recipes for years. She finally did so and compiled them into a family cookbook with a little something added. With each recipe, the woman added a little story about the special times she remembered fixing the recipe, which family member enjoyed the particular recipe the most, and other details around family mealtimes. The woman's history—the life review—was recorded in between what the woman did best. Her family regarded her as a great cook, but now they would also remember her life every time they prepared one of her dishes. This was a great family gift and a very creative way to achieve life review. It is important to remember that life review among the elderly takes place as a normal developmental process. The therapist simply needs to listen in with the aging family as the normal process occurs.

CONCLUSION

Life review is perhaps the most widely used therapy with older people. It is popular because it ties in with our logical belief that as people near the end of life, they tend to want to make sense of the whole affair. From a contextual therapy view, the life review gives a unique opportunity to access information about the past ledger of obligations and entitlements within the family. As the therapist listens to the reminiscences of the aging family, important themes and issues reveal themselves. The therapist can then use this information in determining the best therapeutic interventions for a particular family.

During the life review, the therapist is given further opportunity to validate and be partial to each family member's particular interests. Therefore, it is essential that the therapist maintain the multidirected partiality approach, whether or not all family members are present. Simply stated, each family member has a side or interest in the family history. Also, the life review process is likely to reveal important systemic transactions or communication patterns in the family. The therapist can learn how the family interacts by carefully observing how each member handles information and questions in the context of each other. These observations will also prove useful to the therapist as he or she works to design the therapeutic intervention that holds out the most promise for success with a given family.

III

THERAPEUTIC
INTERVENTIONS

7

MULTIDIRECTED PARTIALITY

There are times when the dysfunction of a family is quite severe and the relational damage it has caused is profound and humbling. As therapists, we have had those experiences of dealing with parents who are physically abusive to their children, only to be shown the scars and be told the horrifying stories of how these parents, as children, were physically abused even more harshly by their own parents. We have seen the rage of adult sons or daughters who were vulnerable as children and were forced to have incestuous relations with a parent for years, sometimes in the presence of the other parent. We have witnessed the insidious damage that invades family relationships as individuals continue drug and alcohol addictions while their families are forced to sever interactions. Perhaps most profound and damaging to the family is when an individual member gives up on the reality of relating altogether and commits a horrible homicide or suicide. But some of the most shocking damage that we have seen as therapists has been with dysfunctional aging families that will at times curse one another for the lack of mutual care and concern and, at the same time, openly wish for one another's death so they can be "free from the emotional burden."

Of course, there is no freedom in this type of relational irresponsibility. Individual entitlements or family obligations that are not met in one generation seem to be perpetuated as a still-open issue in the next. Each generation is just one link in a long gen-

125

erational chain that is empowered or hindered emotionally by the previous generations, just as it is strengthened or weakened by the biological genetic heritage of the previous generations (Boszormenyi-Nagy & Spark, 1984). In our opinion, at no time in the life cycle are the generational linkages and emotional realities more poignant than when the family experiences the reality of old age. To have the eldest generation come to the end of life and have the aging family inflict its last damaging insults on one another in an effort to self-justify individual members is more than sad. Precious emotional resources that are needed for the healthy existence of the family are squandered, and the opportunity is lost forever as the generations pass.

It is into this difficult family arena that the therapist must step and move the family to take advantage of the resources that it commands, instead of perpetuating its dysfunction. It has been our experience that where isolation and loneliness exists in the family, there is a breakdown in the essential trust and justice needed to care for the intergenerational well-being of the family. Existential debt burdens individual members and the family as a whole in isolation as each unit tries to secure entitlement at the expense of others. These individual efforts to correct entitlement imbalances can be as quiet and unobtrusive as refusing to show proper care for one another or as severe and exaggerated as deliberate exploitation of another or imposition of physical harm. But no matter how it is done, when individual members refuse to fulfill their intergenerational familial obligations, they isolate themselves and damage and weaken the next generation's ability to survive.

It is our belief then, that the root of family dysfunction lies in its members' refusal to responsibly execute family obligations. In order to bring about change, the family must build resources. These resources are built when the individual family members again take up the cause of the intergenerational group and meet their obligations to perpetuate the family. Simply stated, individuals in the family begin to give to one another. As a person gives to the family and meets obligations, he or she rightfully earns the reciprocal consideration of others. The giving individual earns merit or is entitled to receive fair consideration of his or her needs and concerns. In short, in order for an individual to receive what he or she needs and deserves, he or she must give. There are, of course, entitlements by factual reality, but in the course of intergenerational family interaction and correcting dysfunction, giving in order to receive is an essential cornerstone.

However, within this important process there is a paradox with which both therapist and client must grapple. In essence, the therapist is trying to motivate individuals in the dysfunctional family to give away the meager resources they have secured for themselves. Asking an aging man to give emotional care and concern to his uncaring and angry daughter is like asking a starving man to give away his last piece of bread. The emotional turmoil and the questions stimulated by the giving are the same. "How will the gift be used?" "Will it be appreciated?" But the most important question the individual will ask will center on "How will I survive and how will I be treated after I give?" These are essential questions of trust. It is extremely difficult to overcome a barrier of distrust if one has never experienced justice or fair consideration from the very person or persons he or she is now being asked to trust. Nevertheless, giving and meeting obligations is the essential element in reciprocal consideration which, in turn, is a necessary component in building the trust that is so integral to leading the family out of dysfunction.

In most problem families, it is necessary for the therapist to initiate the trust-building process. The therapist "primes the pump" with dialogue that affords the therapist an opportunity to credit and be partial to each individual's concern. This process of crediting and partiality is called multidirected partiality, and it should always be employed in addressing the relational ethical concerns of the family. However, there are times when the multidirected partiality functions as the intervention with the family. The purpose of this chapter is to explore this technique as an intervention.

THE TECHNIQUE OF MULTIDIRECTED PARTIALITY

We often think of multidirected partiality in terms of balancing a broom in the air. If one holds the broom upside down with the stick in his or her hand, one can maintain the balance for quite a while using only one hand, provided several factors are employed. First, the person must use his or her senses to determine and anticipate the imbalance of the broom head. Second, the person must counteract the imbalance of the broom with slow and oscillating motion from side to side. If the person ever stops the movement, the broom will become imbalanced and fall to one side. Balance is maintained by motion. It is this "balance in motion" (Van Heusden & Van Den Eerenbeemt, 1987) that is the essential core of contextual relationships. Intergenerational relationships are in a constant state of dynamic equilibrium as individual entitlements and family obligations are balanced throughout the passage of time. In order to be partial to individual and family concerns, the therapist must use his or her senses to determine imbalances and then counteract the imbalance with his or her therapeutic motion.

We argue that the therapeutic motion achieved by this technique of multidirected partiality is the most powerful intervention tool used in therapy with aging families. As the therapist acknowledges each family member's entitlement, individuals are taught how to utilize the same resource in relationships between each other (Boszormenyi-Nagy & Krasner, 1986). Members are recognized for their "side" as well as being held responsible for crediting other members' "sides." Giving consideration and partiality to other family members' concerns is then the most elemental part of giving in the family, and it serves as the initial step in trust-building. When family members start this giving, it signals that the relationships are in a state of rejunction and that members will begin the hard task of acknowledging their own irresponsibility and unfair actions. This further consideration and exploration of intergenerational relations builds family resources. Giving begets more trust and trust begets more giving in a spiralling reciprocation of stronger family relations (Boszormenyi-Nagy & Ulrich, 1981).

Boszormenyi-Nagy and Krasner (1986) define multidirected partiality as the therapist's commitment to help everyone in his or her relational world. This partiality eventually leads to a redistribution of family burdens and benefits and thereby shifts transactions and roles. Ultimately, all family members yield beneficial returns from the trustworthy dialogue and changes initiated by multidirected partiality. Several aspects of multidirected partiality are identified as being important in the therapeutic process (Boszormenyi-Nagy & Krasner, 1986).

Empathy

Empathy is the openness of the therapist to imagine the feeling mode of each family member as he or she identifies his or her own personal perspective on individual entitlements and family obligations. It is important to remember that in the relational reality, even destructive behavior that abuses an innocent party has an element of self-justifying behavior on the abuser's part. In other words, all family members have some definition of justice as a goal in their interactions and behaviors. Being empathetic means that the therapist must at least acknowledge the feelings and conflict each individual feels in the relationship—even when that individual might be destructive in the relationship. For instance, it may be revolting to the therapist to see an adult child verbally abuse an elder parent who has serious physical ailments. However, the therapist can still empathize in recognizing the emotional burden the adult child is carrying and perhaps the feelings that he or she has concerning the parent's previous lack of care and nurturing. The therapist need not condone improper or destructive relational behavior in order to empathize with the underlying reasons for it.

Crediting

Crediting is more clearly a contextual therapy concept. Basically, crediting is acknowledging justice or injustice in the balance of individual entitlements and family obligations. In crediting, the therapist acknowledges that if placed in the same situations, other people might take the same actions or have the same feelings that are experienced by the individual family member. Crediting acknowledges the individual and family sense of justice as individual members deal with the conflict between give and take. For instance, an elderly woman who was in poor physical health demanded that her son care for her and allow her to live with his family. The son refused because of his job responsibility and the elderly woman became depressed. But when questioned, the woman revealed that in her preretirement years, she had given up a job she loved in order to care for both her mother and her husband's mother. She felt the move to care for her family isolated her from her career and friends; now she felt she was isolated from the care she deserved. Crediting acknowledges this woman's perspective on the conflict and imbalance in the give and take of entitlements and obligations.

Of course, the therapist can never fully understand the intergenerational ledger of credits and debits in the family give and take. The family itself must act as the ultimate jury with regard to justice and fairness in the family. But the therapist who has an understanding of basic humanity and the specific family background and history through the life validation and life review has the ability to give credit and to encourage other family members to give credit.

Expectation

A therapist also shows partiality by the expectation that family members are able to show care and to act differently toward one another. For instance, an angry daughter may resent her aging mother's long-standing drug addiction and her irresponsible parenting when the daughter was young. The mother, on the other hand, may acknowledge that she is and was as addicted and irresponsible as the daughter claims and sees little that she can do to change now. The therapist's expectation that both mother and daughter explore new ways of relating in a trustworthy fashion holds the mother to a new relational responsibility. It also encourages the daughter to give up negative expectations and to explore ways that new behavior on the mother's part can serve to expiate the past. Partiality, in this instance, demonstrates to the mother the expectation that she will now be able to show care and concern to the daughter in effective and responsible ways. Expectation shows partiality to the daughter in that the therapist believes she can give up old issues and to accept the mother's effort to make significant changes designed to redress injustices.

Inclusiveness

Inclusiveness represents the therapist's commitment that every family member's relational perspective will get a fair hearing and the therapist will side with his or her perspective. It ensures that all family members' concerns and conflicts will be treated equally and with respect. Also, inclusiveness on the therapist's part shows partiality in that it gives notice to all family members that one person's concerns will not receive consideration at the expense of other individuals in the family. In short, inclusiveness serves as a guarantee to the family that the therapist will not join in with any scapegoating of individual members.

Timing

In the course of being partial and giving fair consideration to each family member, sequence and timing are important. Some family members may have suffered more injury than others throughout the family life cycle. The presenting problem of the aging family may demand that the therapist address that issue first and the views of the parties who are most connected to the problem. At times, because of the intergenerational nature of the family, it may become necessary to be partial to generations in succession from oldest to youngest or youngest to oldest.

It is important for the therapist to remember that multidirected partiality is designed to build relational resources of balance and trust. Therefore, the therapist's intuition about what issues will help the family build resources to tackle even tougher family issues becomes an important aspect of timing. Finally, resources are maximized in the family when the therapist utilizes partiality in recognition of each individual's entitlement. Dysfunctional aging families, like other families, will often want to focus on the destructive behavior of one member. Focusing partiality on what each family member deserves instead of wrongs perpetrated by the family is essential in determining pacing and timing.

CASE EXAMPLE: KEEPING THE SON OCCUPIED

Multidirected partiality, when performed correctly as a therapeutic intervention, is a tough and forward-thrusting action. Partiality is not impartiality or neutrality (Boszormenyi-Nagy & Ulrich, 1981). Being impartial or neutral in the face of an aging family's conflict does nothing to improve accountability or resources. Once the therapist has invited and received an individual member's side of the conflict between give and take, there is an increasing demand that the other family members respond in a constructive fashion and that they give proper recognition to the individual's position (Boszormenyi-Nagy & Ulrich, 1981). In this way, the therapist is the driving force of multidirected partiality that flows to the family and increases pressure on the family to respond with courage and integrity (Boszormenyi-Nagy & Krasner, 1986). Multidirected partiality, when successful, starts with the therapist exploring tough relational issues and gradually moves into the family members' exploring issues and being partial to one another's positions on their own.

In the following case example, an 82-year-old widow was spitting in the halls, common sitting areas, and dining room of the personal care facility in which she was living. As her cognitive abilities were in the normal range, her refusal to comply with repeated requests that she control her unacceptable behavior suggested that there was another reason for the spitting. In the first several sessions of therapy, the life validation stage revealed that the woman was the youngest child of a large family and was the family favorite. When she married, she was very dependent upon her husband. Because of her small size and girlish mannerisms, she and the rest of her family reported that she was treated like a child by others. Her only son was her primary caregiver since her husband had died. In the first therapy session with both the mother and son present, the frustration of the spitting problem is evident.

Therapist: It seems to be a difficult problem that is hard to figure out.

Mother: Well, it's probably just a habit I guess.

Son: Well you can use a tissue or something, but you just can't spit on the floor.

Mother: (angrily) Well I don't spit on the floor all the time!

Son: But that's what the problem is. I see to it that you have plenty of tissues. That's not the problem. You can use anything but you can't spit on the floor. I can imagine what you would have done to me if I would have spit on the floor of your house when I was a kid.

Mother: I would have killed you. (with a smile) Naw, I really wouldn't have.

Son: But you would have been really upset. You probably would have hit me. Should we hit you? That's not acceptable and that wouldn't do any good anyway.

Therapist: You brought up a good point. What would you have done to him?

Mother: Well I wouldn't like it.

Son: Remember Aunt Mae's house? When I was a little boy and I spit on the floor of her house, what would you have done to me?

Mother: I would have hit you.

Son: Absolutely. And why would you have hit me?

Mother: Because you spit on the floor. Especially at someone else's house.

Son: So you know you're not suppose to do it?

Mother: I know.

Son: Then why do you spit on the floor?

Many problems with older people and aging families have symptomatology such as somatic illness, constant complaining, depression, or—as demonstrated here—unacceptable behavior. The mother probably had taken a dependent role all her life and was the focus of family attention. This developed transactional patterns in the family that supported her dependent position. In this last interchange, we can see how the son scolds his mother much in the same way an adult would scold a child. Even the effort to reason with the mother indicates that this mother has engaged in childish behavior for a long time leading up to this problem. As is often the case with aging families, individual members often assume that the personality of the aging member will not change and transactional patterns of the past become even more entrenched. The mother knows that she should not spit on the floor, but the son insists on demanding in a parental fashion that she not spit. The old roles of the mother and son are therefore further supported by this unsuccessful transaction.

Later in the session the son revealed that the mother and his wife never had a good relationship because the mother would interfere with the son's family life and be too dependent. Although the conflict had been covert for years, the son obviously felt a split loyalty as he was between the two women. The son's wife was now quite ill. The therapist hypothesized that the mother felt entitled to her dependent position in the family and the spitting behavior was a destructive method to ensure that the son would be forced to take care of her instead of taking care of his wife. In the next session with just the mother present, the therapist tests this hypothesis by empathizing with the mother's feelings and placing the expectation on her to help the family. Notice how the therapist extends partiality to other family members even though they are not present in the session.

Therapist: It seems to be a very sad time for the family with your son's wife being so sick.

Mother: It is a very sad time. I hope that nothing bad happens. I just don't want anything bad to happen to anyone.

Therapist: It is hard for you to see your family go through this?

Mother: It is hard because I don't know, they don't know what will happen.

Therapist: I agree. It must be very difficult for your son, your grandchildren, and your daughter-in-law to live with the pressure of this sickness. Are there ways that you can be strong for the family when bad things happen?

Mother: How could I be strong for the family? Tell me and I'll do it. I'll show it on the inside.

Therapist: One of the things that might help is you and your son's wife would talk a little more often. Maybe you could eventually get a little closer.

Mother: How could we get closer? I hardly ever see her. If I had a car, I could drive over and see her. I guess I could try and get a car.

Here is evidence again of the mother's entrenchment in her dependent role in the family. The mother not only was incapable of driving because of her age, she had never learned to drive. Her suggestion that she could get a car and visit her son's wife is a clear indication to the therapist that she is afraid to give serious consideration to being a support to the family and changing her dependent role. The therapist holds the mother to the expectation that she should do something that would strengthen the family unit. Although this is again resisted by the mother, she finally agrees to make some contribution.

Therapist: Well since you don't drive, what could you do instead?
Mother: I could pray for her. That would help. It helps a lot.
Therapist: It would be nice if your son's wife knew that you were praying for her.
Therapist: Yes. Well, I'll tell my son to tell her that I will pray for her.
Therapist: I'm going to make the suggestion that you should tell her yourself.
Mother: Well I don't ever see her face to face.
Therapist: Maybe then your could communicate by letter.
Mother: I could, but I hate to write. Maybe I'll just give her a call.
Therapist: (moving to solidify the mother's commitment to call) Well, you could call, but a letter is so much more meaningful because it is harder to write than just talk. Your son's wife would know how difficult it would be for you to write and so it would be more meaningful. But at any rate, you can decide if you call or write.
Mother: I'll just call her.

The therapist's expectation was that if the mother could address the daughter-in-law directly, the issues between the two would have to be addressed. The son would no longer have to function in a split loyalty role because his wife and his mother would deal with one another. As expected, the mother never did call the daughter-in-law. However, the spitting behavior did stop. After three weeks of no spitting, the therapy was ended. Within two weeks, the spitting behavior resurfaced. It was likely that as the mother was relieved from the expectation of communicating with the daughter-in-law, she felt unhindered in the self-justifying claim on her son.

It was further hypothesized by the therapist that the spitting behavior was a means of protecting the son from the pain of dealing with his wife's illness. Since this mother had always been dependent, there was little constructive option open to her to care and nurture her son's grief. Also, she obviously had relational concerns that she would not be cared for if the son became too consumed with his wife's illness. The mother, even though she acted as a dependent child, was still a mother and had all the concerns that a mother would have for a grieving son. The spitting behavior perhaps served as a destructive claim that the mother was at once dependent and wanting to help assuage the son's grief.

In the next session with the mother and son present, the therapist uses multidirected partiality in stimulating dialogue, empathy, and responsibility. This partiality was aimed at giving the mother a constructive means of addressing the son's grief and giving the son the freedom to allow his mother not to be dependent in this area.

Therapist: (to the son) Is there a time when you wanted to show care for someone but didn't quite know how?

Son: Yeah. When I was in Korea and was away from my wife and kids. I thought about them everyday and worried about them. All I could think of was getting home. I spent too much of my time being unhappy because I wasn't with my family.

Therapist: Why was it that you wanted to get home so bad?

Son: I missed my wife—my children—I hated to see them grow up without me. I worried about them all the time.

Therapist: I wonder if your mother worries about you the way you worried about your wife and kids.

Mother: (seriously) I sure do.

Therapist: In what way do you worry?

Mother: Well, I just worry. I know he is a good kid. He won't do anything to hurt me. I love him. I love his children.

Therapist: It seems difficult for your mother to say exactly what she worries about.

Son: (to the mother) Are you worried about being alone?

Mother: Yes. I hate to be alone.

Son: I know how it is being alone. I totally understand. You can be in a room full of people and be alone. I don't know what to tell you to do. Just get other interests. (pause) You were so dependent on your husband, my father. You were totally dependent on him.

Mother: That's right.

Son: See, you know that. And now you transferred that dependence to me.

Mother: And you can't take care of me because of your wife—but not your children because they are all grown.

Son: That's right. They are grown and I don't worry about them anymore. Well, a little bit I worry about them. They are not on my mind continually.

The relational conflict of the interests of the mother and son become very evident. The mother worries about the son, but only can express her concern in terms of asking for reassurance that the son will take care of her. The son first responds to the mother in the old fashion by acknowledging her fear that he will not care for her. But as the son empathizes with the mother's loneliness, he talks honestly about the dependency of the mother, which in turn spurs more empathy with her worry.

Therapist: This is difficult. She's your mother, but you have to take care of her. She's worried about you, but she has difficulty expressing her concern because she is dependent. So it comes out that she is worried that you won't take care of her. But I feel she is worried about you.

Son: (to the mother) Well, don't be worried. (laughingly) That really is an empty statement—don't worry. Really an empty statement. I understand that. But what is going to be is going to be.

Therapist: One of the things you discussed with me is your son's wife.

Mother: I am so worried about her. She is so sick. I hope that she gets well real soon.

Son: Well she's not going to get well. You can just forget that. She's just not going to get well.

Mother: Are you worried about her?

Son: Well—no—you know, there is nothing I can really do about it. You just have to learn to accept it. You just have to take one day at a time. Like giving up smoking. You never smoked but I did. You just quit one day at a time. (pause) It was a funny thing. One day last year I wanted a cigarette and I have not smoked since 1958. Of course I didn't get one.

Therapist: One of those things you never forget.

Son: That's right. (then turning to the mother) Like you never forget that I am your kid and so you worry about me. What can I say. I do know this though, that you have got to quit spitting on the floor.

The mother makes real progress in this interchange as she faces the fact that the wife is seriously ill. She makes an initial effort to question the son on an adult level about his concern for his wife. However, the son rejects his mother's offer to show care and concern for him by listening to his pain. The story of the cigarette is clearly a metaphor about the son knowing that this is a key moment. He indicates that he can change and do something out of character or he can remain steadfast. For the time being, he indicates that he will remain steadfast with old relationships by turning the potentially trust-building situation back to focus on the spitting behavior.

Therapist: You say that there is just nothing that you can do about your wife. Does your mother know how that makes you feel not to be able to do anything? It must be tough seeing this happen.

Son: Well you never met my wife, but she is a very tough individual—I mean mentally tough. This is a woman who goes to the dentist and does not get novocain when she has a simple filling. She is very hardy. She raised four kids because I was gone a large part of the time during our marriage. She was 19 when we got married. She went back to college and got her degree. She is very intelligent.

Mother: I was very proud of her.

Son: It is like living with someone—I might have had influence on her when she was younger but I don't have much influence now. She does what she wants to do. That's good because it takes much of the burden off of me. She is directed. She knows. She has accepted this disease far more than I do. She reads about it all the time.

Therapist: That's often the case. It is harder for the ones who will be left than the one who will pass on. Physical pain is one thing, but emotional pain is tough.

Son: Just last weekend we had plans. She felt terrible. She said that she could stay home and feel bad or go and feel bad and maybe have some fun. So she went. That's her attitude. When I am sick, I want to stay home.

Therapist: She is a tough person. (then turning to the mother) How did you comfort your son when he was a boy?

Mother: I would love on him and his daddy would love on him and try to help him when he was sad.

Son: (joking) I don't think I was ever sad was I?

Mother: (seriously) Not very much.

Son: (now serious) Of course, I do think you reject the sad things.

The son takes the opportunity to explain how difficult it is for him to face his wife's illness. By overemphasizing her toughness, the son is perhaps revealing his relational difficulty in expressing his feelings in his marital relationship. When the therapist offers the opportunity for the mother to recount a caring time, she recounts comfort she gave when her son was sad, which he obviously is now. The son first rejects the mother's care with a joke. This time, however, the mother stays with the effort by keeping a serious tone, which in turn forces the son to reciprocate by acknowledging that he rejects many of the sad things he feels.

Therapist: So you still worry about him.

Mother: Oh yes. The same way that you worry about your wife and children.

Therapist: You are right. I do worry about them. (to both mother and son) You are a mother who worries about your son. You are a son who takes care of your mother and who has a sick wife. How can you show care for your son now that he is not a little boy—he is a grown man that takes care of you. Everybody in the family seems to be tough. How do you show care? Seems to me that nobody in the family needs a caring grandmother.

Son: (both mother and son acknowledge the correctness of the statement) So maybe you don't feel that anyone needs you because you can't cook or anything.

Mother: I can't cook. I use to.

Son: Absolutely. So you don't feel that anyone needs you?

Mother: My mind isn't all there.

Son: Well, I have trouble with my mind too. I forget things too. Sometimes I feel . . .

Mother: (interrupting) Lonely, huh?

Son: No, you feel lonely.

The mother demonstrates that she completely understands the son's loneliness even though the son again rejects her empathy. However, the son and mother are now clearly using the dialogue to credit one another's positions in the family and the difficulty and conflict each one feels.

Therapist: Do you worry about him being lonely?

Mother: (pausing and looking at the son for a cue) No. He's a big
    guy and he can take care of himself.

Therapist: So maybe he doesn't need a mother to give him comfort
    in a tough time?

Mother: He doesn't need to be babied.

Therapist: But still people need a place to fit to show they care.

Son: Well where do other older people fit in the family. I don't
    think anyone else spits on the floor. (after a long pause, very
    tenderly) You know, even if my wife were to die, you still
    could not live with me. There is just no way. You will have
    to live on your own.

Mother: I know that.

While the two did not formulate a complete role for the mother,
the multidirected partiality provides each with an opportunity to
express personal positions and concerns honestly. During these discussions, some steps were taken toward building trust between
mother and son, and both people clearly demonstrated that they
were capable and willing to at times empathize with one another,
credit one another's relational conflicts, and expect one another
to respond in a new fashion. Certainly, each became more delineated as the dialogues progressed and both parent and child were
able to respond in an increasingly honest fashion. Many of the feelings are expressed through metaphor and projection, but still the
feelings are the subject of conversation. The son suggested at the
end of the session that it would be helpful if there were continued
meetings between the mother and son. This is a clear indication
that the partiality shown in the session was helpful to him and
was seen as improving the relationship. In the next session, the
therapist again talked about the concern in the family.

Therapist: What do you do when you worry about your wife?

Son: I don't know that I do anything. I just put it out of my mind.

I work or watch television. You live with things. How does my wife live with this? I have no idea. She is tough.

Therapist: Does she talk about her illness with you?

Son: Oh yes. We talk about it. She's read all the literature about the disease. She wants me to read it and I don't.

Therapist: Out of the things that you do to support your wife at this time, what is the most important thing?

Son: Probably the most important thing I do is listen to her.

Therapist: Who listens to you?

Son: (laughing) Well, I have a few pals at work. Sometimes we talk.

Therapist: I wonder if your mother could listen to you.

Mother: I sure could.

Son: I don't know. Maybe she could.

As long as the mother and son continued the therapy sessions, the spitting behavior stopped. After eight additional sessions, the mother and son agreed to discuss their family concerns together without the help of the therapist. The spitting behavior resurfaced only sporadically when the mother and son would not meet together on a regular basis. Although the mother was still significantly dependent upon her son, she shifted her destructive behavior in response to the son's grief to a constructive concern that empowered the son.

CONCLUSION

This case demonstrates that multidirected partiality can be a powerful intervention tool with the family. When the therapist uses partiality, he or she models the constructive dialogue that builds trust and reinforces resources in family relationships. As with this family, the individuals start slowly to acknowledge one another's relational positions and empathize with one another, which facilitates the building of trust that eventually leads to individuals being able to respond differently in the family. The mother in this case has been dependent all her life, but she has a legitimate concern for her son. Partiality encourages her to explore new resources to express that concern to her son and to offer him loving care. Her desire to listen to her son's grief is evidence that she wishes to be a resource and not a burden to her son. Although she remained dependent on her son in many areas, this listening was a great gift that contributed to the intergenerational survival of the family facing the death of an important member.

8

EXONERATION, FORGIVENESS, AND HEALING IN THE FAMILY

The human body has the unique and wonderful ability to heal itself. All of us have had minor cuts or scrapes that healed within a matter of days and have long been forgotten because they left no visible trace. We all have fallen victim to common infections and viruses, which our bodies have gone on to fight and eventually overcome successfully. Other damage to the body can be more severe, with wounds that are too deep or pronounced to heal without a scar. Some damage cannot be repaired, and we may feel its effects for the rest of our lives.

Healing in the intergenerational family is much the same. When parents and children live together over many years, it is quite normal that interpersonal and intergenerational hurts occur. Most of these hurts are quite minor and forgiveness and healing are quick to occur and leave no permanent scars. Other hurts are more serious. Healthy, flexible families tend to deal with these wounds in appropriate, caring ways, without undue delay between the wound and the reconciliation called for by the family hurt. Scars may be left by some of these wounds, but they usually do not damage the family functioning and the family is able to adapt in appropriate ways.

Still, there are other relational hurts in the family that are so severe that they challenge relational existence. When major damage is done in relationships, it seems that smaller hurts only serve to exasperate the major hurt. Like the body with a major illness, relational survival is in question. Healing requires the family to resolve the hurt through a tough and complicated process of exoneration and forgiving. Forgiving is hard work for even the strongest and most willing of families. Some families, however, are unable or unwilling to pursue this healing process. Over years, then, the wounds and the hurts tend to accumulate and grow in an unforgiving or distant family atmosphere; family relationships may suffer a slow, agonizing death. Damage is inflicted and left unrepaired, and then is passed on to the next generation.

This chapter examines some family traumas and helps situate family pain in the framework of contextual family therapy. Then, the outline for the hard work of exoneration and forgiveness is delineated. Finally, the chapter presents a clinical example that illustrates the efficacy of a contextual family therapy approach in dealing with family pain.

FAMILY PAIN

Certainly pain can be caused in a family by various factors. Nature can hurt a family—genetic accidents, incurable diseases, tornadoes or earth-quakes—so much is beyond our control. Systems can also do a family harm. A government may deal harshly with a family simply based on the color of their skin or cultural background. Economic systems may stymie a family's potential to better the lot of its offspring (Smedes, 1984).

However, as Smedes (1984) points out, it is only people who can be held accountable in relationships and who can give and accept forgiveness. Forgiveness is necessary when we are hurt or wronged by a person we trusted to treat us right. It does not matter if the person who opened the wound treated us unfairly by design or unintentionally; the hurt has the same effect. Relational pain in the family is the consequence of injustice: a trusted member who fails to fulfill fair obligations or who forces, manipulates, or uses others to fulfill obligations that are not his or her responsibility.

Family therapists have long known that many families come to therapy at critical transition points in the life of the family such as the first year of marriage, as the couple attempts to separate from respective families of origin; at the birth of their first child; when the children enter school; when the children become adolescents and begin to plan to leave home; when all the children are gone and the older couple is once more alone; when one or both adults retire from working full time.

Many of these clinical families are stuck in some normal developmental transition point; often, the family is rigid and unable to cope with these growth points and the changes that they require of everyone in the family system. When conflicts occur and are not resolved, there are scars left behind. They become imbedded in the family system, often remaining there for many years or even generations. Common symptoms that may suggest the presence of unresolved issues can form: coolness in intergenerational family relationships, withdrawal or even complete cutoffs, anger and hostility, and acting out by one or more of the family members— abuse, addiction, or scapegoating.

In her recent book on intergenerational adult relationships, Smith (1991) has noted harmful patterns and traumatic situations that can characterize intergenerational families in pain. Some of the more common family wounds over years include the following:

Physical Mistreatment

Usual forms of physical mistreatment include violence such as severe spanking, burning, choking, and hitting with belts or other objects, as well as other assertions of power such as force feeding and restricting mobility. In families where no forgiveness was asked or given after physical mistreatment, the intergenerational ledger remains severely unbalanced. These scars remain with people many years after they have moved into adulthood. The adult children still feel the effects of such treatment, and they want the aging parent to make amends for the lack of respectful parenting.

Emotional Mistreatment

Emotional mistreatment encompasses a range of behaviors including name-calling, violent outbursts, invasion of privacy, perfectionism, overcontrol, excessive criticism, and parentification of the child. Children raised in a family with this kind of abuse often become adults with little sense of personal autonomy and with low self-esteem. As adults, these people may distance themselves from their aging parents to protect themselves from regressing to a helpless child in the presence of either the father or mother. Nevertheless, these individuals may still yearn for affirmation from the aging parent.

Neglect

Neglect usually shows itself in patterns of insufficient physical or emotional nurturing, deprivation of the essentials of life (food, shelter, clothing), poor communication, or extended absences. Children who have suffered from neglect often have serious problems as adults in developing close, intimate relationships. Often they are drawn as adults to significant partners who in fact do not provide the close relationship they crave. These adult children have difficulty in moving closer to their aging, dying parents, as their life-long fear of being neglected by the parents overwhelms the urge to draw closer to them. Contextual family therapists believe that if such reconciliation does not take place, the unbalanced family ledger will be passed down to the next generations.

Addictions

Common addictions include alcohol, other drugs, food (eating disorders), and a variety of other excessive attachments (i.e., exercise, religion, work, spending, and gambling). Parental addictions, especially if they are severe and long-standing, can have serious repercussions for the children. Such children see their parents as putting the addiction before them. Thus, in such families, neglect and mistreatment of the children are very common, much to the detriment of the nurturance of the children.

Sexual Abuse

Sexual abuse in families can take a variety of forms: sexual overstimulation, inappropriate touching, masturbation, oral or anal sex, intercourse, or not protecting the child from sexual abuse. Therapists have long known the pernicious effects on an adult of being sexually abused as a child. Trust with anyone, especially with intimates, is extremely difficult. Those who experience such abuse often experience much confusion and fear about their own gender identity and their capacity for a satisfying sexual relationship with another adult.

Other Wounds

Other familial situations that can traumatize children: a family atmosphere that is tense, harsh, or cold; secrets and lying; affairs, divorces and separations; scapegoating the child; and family systems that are either extremely enmeshed or disengaged.

THE CONTEXTUAL VIEW OF INTERGENERATIONAL FAMILY PAIN

The contextual family therapist recognizes the existence of family pain, so acutely felt by those adult children who grew up in dysfunctional families; there, harmful patterns and traumatic situations were the rule, rather than the exception. The deep scars—physical, emotional, and interpersonal—are indeed very real to these adult children, who often desperately seek some resolution of the hurt before the aging parents die.

According to contextual family therapy, where there is a severe violation of entitlement or obligation in the intergenerational family system, distrust can, and usually does, result. This systemic distrust tends to drain family members of their willingness to give to each other. Adults who were abused as children can then be faced with the approaching death of the elderly parents, without the healing of the intergenerational trauma. If this healing does not occur, the adult children may look for some sort of intergenerational retribution. This retribution usually occurs at the expense of their own children, who then become the next generation of abused offspring.

However, when the intergenerational family can talk openly about the real or imagined hurts of the past, the family members then have the opportunity to set the past right by mutual giving to each other. Boszormenyi-Nagy and Spark (1984) state:

> No matter how vindictive a person may have felt or still feels, the therapeutic goal is not mere recognition, confrontation, open expression, and thus a continuation of the negative relationships, but is focused on mutual clarification and reconstruction. The adult child and his parent are provided an opportunity to break destructive chainlike patterns of relationships which may have continued for several generations.
>
> The children are so keenly aware that their relationships with their own parents could be much more openly loving and giving, if their parents could resolve some of their conflicts with the grandparents. In one family, the parents spoke with ridicule and contempt for their aged parents and then had difficulty tying to figure out why their own children mocked and ridiculed them! (pp. 227–228)

Boszormenyi-Nagy and Krasner (1986) describe this process as *exoneration*. Exoneration is the effort of the child who has experienced injustice or hurt from a parent to lift the load of culpability off the parent. Instead of subjecting the parent to endless condemnation, exoneration recognizes the parent's circumstances and past injustices experienced in the family. The child seeks to understand or appreciate the parent's situation, past options, efforts, and limits. They point out that exoneration differs from forgiveness in that forgiveness retains the assumption of guilt of the parent instead of recognizing the parent's victimization. They continue by stating that the forgiving party simply refrain from holding the parent accountable and demanding punishment.

THE WORK OF EXONERATION AND FORGIVENESS

We differ from most contextual therapists in that we believe that exoneration is a step toward forgiveness and that forgiveness is a necessary part of healing relational hurts. We also believe that whether or not the parent or family member is a victim of injustices, that person is still responsible ethically to the intergenerational ledger of relationships. Exoneration is useful in understanding the dynamics and situation of the intergenerational ledger and perhaps it prevents bitterness and dysfunctional patterns from being passed to the next generation; however, guilt that results from family relational injustices cannot be exonerated completely unless accountability is accepted. There simply must be a willingness by both parties to commit to the idea that the relational injustices will never happen again. In other words, because the wrongdoer agrees that he or she was responsible for an injustice that caused hurt or pain, a claim is established that states that if given the same situation, he or she will not perpetrate the hurt again. This in turn allows the wronged person to reestablish a trustworthy relationship with the person. No longer does the wronged person have to hold the wrongdoer responsible; the wrongdoer holds him- or herself responsible. The relationship can continue because responsibility and trust are reestablished.

Still, we feel that exoneration and forgiveness are on the same road. Both are acts of giving in the family that earn entitlement. Since forgiveness is perhaps the toughest work of love (Smedes, 1984), it stands to reason that there are different stations in the process of forgiveness. In working with aging families, we see four distinct stations that work in the process of forgiveness. The first two seem to fit more with exoneration, whereas the latter two fit more with forgiveness.

Station One: Insight

Hurts that are left untreated can fester to cause enormous long-term pain. Severe relational injustices that are repeated over a long period of time can result in powerful and demanding emotions such as guilt, anger, depression, and rage. These emotions can dominate a person's perspective so much that he or she takes destructive action against an innocent party. Most of us, at one time or another, find ourselves repeating harmful phrases or doing hurtful things that were once done to us by our family that we swore we would never do.

Insight is the first station of forgiveness in that it allows a person to see the mechanisms that have caused the damage and hurt. In short, insight brings the hurt or pain to the level of consciousness where an individual can be motivated to not allow the pain to dominate. Bitterness can be a consuming fire. Insight gives a person the ability to step back and see just how the fire gets started and how one can avoid getting burned. In aging families, insight may be helpful in recognizing manipulative phrases or emotional demands that restrict the adult child to a caretaking role. Inconsiderate and unjustified actions by an aging parent may prompt retaliation by an adult child. The ability to see and articulate how the pain has occurred in the past means that a person can guard against the injustice in the future. Although in many cases a relational distance will result, insight at least gives the members of a relationship protection from future harm.

Insight reduces the chances of manipulation and retaliation and therefore actively helps the family members in their effort to contribute to one another and prevent the injustices and imbalances from being passed along to future generations. Insight is limited in its ability to heal relationships because it is used primarily as protection. However, it provides a first important step along the road of reestablishing relational justice by putting the brakes on additional damage.

Station Two: Understanding

Some people stop at the first station of insight to deal with family pain. Others will move to a deeper level of understanding. Understanding differs from insight in that insight specifies how the damage and pain occurs, understanding specifies why they occur. First, understanding seeks to identify the circumstances in which the wrongdoer existed. For instance, an adult child might understand how the parent put too much emotional responsibility on him or her growing up because the parent was immature or was in an unsatisfactory marital relationship. Second, understanding seeks to learn about the injustices that occurred to the wrong doer. Many abused adult children become receptive to understanding when they learn that their own parents were abused in dramatic and dreadful ways. Injustice occurs in all relationships at one time or another. Understanding how those injustices affected the person who caused hurt or pain holds the potential of reducing the pain. The following statement from a middle-aged man clarifies this relationship.

> "My mother always considered herself a good mother and I never could understand how she could say that. She was a terrible mother. She abused us kids. But when she began to tell of the awful abuse she suffered from her father and

mother—much worse than she gave to us—I could see how she was a good mother compared to them. She did the best she could."

Finally, understanding seeks to identify with the wrongdoer and acknowledges that if placed in the same situation from the same background, the wronged person might make the same mistakes and cause the same hurt. We all know that we are fallible; but when we are hurt we tend to place ourselves above others, believing that we could never be responsible for such a wrong. Understanding means that we see the why of hurt and acknowledges that we too have the potential to cause pain. This type of understanding usually alleviates the tendency of the wronged person to blame the wrongdoer. Although it does not remove responsibility, it constructively credits both parties of a relationship by acknowledging different sides of the situation and different injustices. In our experience, both stations of insight and understanding rarely involve addressing the issue of injustice between the parties directly.

Station Three: Giving Opportunity for Compensation

For some people, insight and understanding are enough. Anger and bitterness can be significantly reduced by the first two stations and individuals may be relieved from the burden of transferring the injustice to other relationships. However, insight and understanding are primarily internal responses in the individual psychology of the person who has experienced hurt. The first two stations may establish exoneration of blame for the injustice and pain, but they are not sufficient to reestablish the relationship. We know many people who have insight and understanding toward their families of origin and who have dealt with relational injustices and emotional turmoil, but who choose not to carry on relationships with their families. Reconnection and reestablishment of the trustworthy relational process after severe hurt and pain demand the work of forgiveness.

The third station along the road of forgiveness is giving the wrongdoer the opportunity to compensate for the injustice. This process is distinctly different from waiting for the relational culprit to apologize or entering into the relationship with an eye for future mistakes or injustices. A willingness to allow for compensation means setting aside blame and disdain. It is necessary for the previous two stations of insight and understanding to be negotiated in order for the third to take place. Providing the opportunity for compensation may—or may not—involve addressing the injustice directly. Like a bank giving small credit lines to previously financially irresponsible individuals, the opportunity for compensation means that people who had perpetrated undeserved hurts in the past have a chance to prove themselves again. Trustworthiness is established a little at a time over a long period. But the end result can be the reestablishment of intergenerational trust as individuals prove responsibility and commitment to justice.

What does it mean to give opportunity for compensation? First, it means that one must give up the claim to the injustice. In other words, a person must acknowledge that he or she will accept the effort of the wrongdoer to make the situation right. There are people who have been hurt so severely by someone in their family of origin that they could not imagine anything the person could do to rectify the situation and make the relationship better. Giving up the claim to the injustice means that the wronged person will accept a payment plan on a tremendous debt that has been incurred. We have found that in situations where people were unwilling to accept the effort of the wrongdoer to address the pain and hurt, the pain became a powerful tool used for condemnation, which in turn can lead to manipulation as the undeserved hurt is held over the head of the wrongdoer. Relational destruction is almost always the result.

Second, giving the opportunity for compensation means that a person is willing to open up to the relationship that may once again cause pain. Forgiveness is risky business. People are imperfect and they make mistakes that may result in undeserved hurts. The trusted person who erred and caused great pain may again cause pain. As a result, it has been our observation in therapy that people who have felt wronged might be willing to give the wrongdoer another chance, but they want that person to make the first move. We believe that giving is a prerequisite to any relationship. Therefore, the forgiver must give to the wrongdoer if the relationship is to have a chance to be balanced. We think that a person willing to forgive must fore-give, that is, he or she must be willing to enter into the relationship ready to fulfill the obligations that the relationship would normally demand. This can include setting up the opportunity for the parties to get together, or specifying needs to the other.

Third, giving the opportunity for compensation has to allow for mistakes. When a person is hurt, he or she tends to be overguarded and a bit oversensitive. Any error or misunderstanding in the relationship can send a person into a tailspin of emotional cut-offs and accusations. In giving relationships another chance, a person must always be conscious to keep the small mistakes, that happen in every relationship, small. If not, these small mistakes will feel much like "the straw that broke the camel's back." If simple errors are allowed to cause hurt and pain like the original deed, a person is never able to give up the justification for the original hurt. The bridge of forgiveness cannot be built because some relational mistake always knocks down the work previously constructed. As therapists helping people give opportunity for compensation, we must always seek to provide them with realistic pictures for relational expectations.

Giving the opportunity for compensation between adult children and parents may involve inviting participation in a family tradition or activity. It may involve opening up one's own offspring to relating to grandparents for the first time. But whatever the activity, the people in the relationship work toward forgiveness and trustworthiness by proving justified concern, care, and nurturing for one another. Relational healing can result as severe hurts fade in the face of current trustworthy interactions and care.

Station Four: The Act of Forgiveness

We are often asked the question if one can achieve forgiveness without moving all the way to station four. The answer, we have found, is "yes" or "no," depending on the relationship. We see that forgiveness is always relational—involving at least two people. Responsibility, justice, and trust must all be addressed in achieving forgiveness. It is conceivable to us that these issues can be addressed between people who have hurt one another without having to confront or talk about the issue directly. Time together with the combination of insight, understanding, and giving opportunity to compensate may result in true and heartfelt forgiveness. However, we do feel that forgiveness must have this relational dimension. Individual insight or understanding may serve as a protection device or may stop a dysfunctional family legacy, but it does not achieve forgiveness. Forgiveness takes place between people, not within an individual.

We view the act of forgiveness as having three distinct elements. First, the issue that caused the hurt and pain must be confronted. No matter if the wrongdoer or the wronged person starts this confrontation, the key element in the relationship must be patience and understanding on both sides. Attacks, accusations, counter-accusations, and manipulations do nothing but propel deeper hurts and make future confrontations harder. Therapists must always assist families in approaching conversations about hurt and pain in a positive and impartial way that will promote insight and understanding. Second, there must be acknowledgment of responsibility for the hurt and pain. It has been our experience in therapy with aging families that when the supposed wrongdoer accepted responsibility for the hurt, the wronged person acknowledged his or her relational irresponsibility. Taking responsibility does not mean laying blame on certain family members. Responsibility serves as a stabilizing effort between family members so that they will try to maintain a balanced relationship in the future and guard against hurting one another.

Finally, someone must ask for forgiveness and someone must give it. Again, many times in therapy there is mutual asking and giving between members, even where there seemed to be a clear relational culprit and victim. This final step is important because it releases the charge of the relationship. No longer does the forgiver have to hold the forgiven responsible for the pain. The forgiven will hold him- or herself responsible. Forgiving makes trustworthiness possible once again and this reuniting of the relationship can have phenomenal healing power.

It is important to remember that some hurts will not be forgiven. In some cases, a destructive family member may choose to be destructive in family relationships at every opportunity. Giving the opportunity to compensate for the hurt or moving toward the act of forgiveness may not be possible because it will open individuals up to further abuse and destruction. Some family members refuse to acknowledge responsibility for hurt they have propagated. Other family members, laden with destructive entitlement, will choose not to be forgiven, even with the total cost being loss of relationships. However, we feel that with any family relationship an individual can move somewhere along the road of forgiveness at one of these four stations. Forgiveness is a tough task and may take an individual working through several psychological issues before the relationship can be faced. We have suggested the book *Forgive and Forget* (Smedes, 1984) to many of our clients to help them work through these individual issues preceding relational forgiveness.

Forgiveness is also serious work. Our society speaks the language of forgiveness many times without forgiveness actually being achieved. Many times we have suggested that the act of forgiveness be performed as a family ritual to ensure that the work of forgiveness is realized. A ritual of forgiveness may take the form of asking forgiveness on bended knee, or of the involved parties bury-ing a symbolic representation of the "hurt" the relationship has caused. It has been our experience that rituals, whatever their design, make the act of forgiveness more powerful and meaningful in the family.

CASE EXAMPLE: THE FLY CAUGHT IN THE SPIDER'S WEB

Pain in an aging family may be the result of any number of factors. Some pain may be long term in nature and may have its roots in years of stressful and dysfunctional relationships. Other pain may be the result of specific acts such physical abuse, lies, or deceptive actions. In either case, the contextual family therapist conceptual-izes pain and hurt in the family as being both in individual family members and in the intergenerational family system. The reso-lution of these hurts, therefore, must involve the significant family members, not just the one person who complains about his or her own pain.

In the following example, an 87-year-old widow was taken from her home in a small town and placed in the personal care facility. Her three well-meaning daughters, believing that the mother would never agree to move on her own volition, told the mother that they were taking her to visit one of the daughters. They feared that the mother was no longer able to take care of her basic needs because of her failing memory, deteriorating health, and improper diet. Without the mother's knowledge, they had arranged for the mother to live at the personal care home. Once they arrived there, the daughters revealed their intention for the mother to stay there on a permanent basis. The mother was very upset and became depressed. This situation in the family produced vast amounts of injustice and distrust leading to constant bickering and name-calling among family members. The level of tension in the family was evident in this conversation between the mother and the youn-gest daughter.

Mother: What did I say?

Daughter: Well, you have been saying some pretty hurtful things. Calling us painful names that hurt pretty deeply ...

Mother: (interrupting) Well, you deserve it! You deserve it! All of you framed up on me.

Therapist: I know they have hurt you because of their dishonesty.

Mother: I don't care. I can live without them if I have to. They have hurt me. They put me in here. I didn't know what I was getting into. I walked in here just like a fly who gets caught in a spider's web! This is a big town and I'm used to a small town. Now I'm stuck here and I can't extricate myself.

The daughters' actions, even though they were motivated by love and concern for their mother's health, violated the sense of respect and honesty the mother felt she deserved. On the other hand, the mother's refusal to allow any action or conversation on the subject of her declining health put the daughters into a double bind. They were backed into the situation of having to choose between respect for their mother's wishes or providing proper care for her. After exploring the background of the case in the first four sessions using the techniques of life validation and life review, the therapist moves the family to the point of intervention aimed at restimulating justice and trust. The first step in the intervention was to ask the youngest daughter, who was closest to the mother, to reckon with and ask forgiveness for kidnapping the mother from her home.

Therapist: Perhaps what is needed is forgiveness.

Daughter: I think we need forgiveness on both sides so we can pick up the pieces and go on from here. There is too much love between us.

Therapist: What do you need to forgive her for?

Daughter: For some of the terrible things she has said to us.

Mother: (angrily) I'll tell you something. I can get along by myself
    whether I ever see these kids again!
Therapist: Could you let your mother go?
Daughter: I don't think so.
Therapist: Tell her why.
Mother: That's just it. You tried to do it your way and not mine.
    It doesn't make any difference. I have just a few years left
    anyway!
Daughter: But mother, those years can be rewarding. I want you
    here safe and healthy.
Therapist: That is understandable. But do you think that taking
    her from her home without her knowledge was the right
    thing?
Daughter: I don't think it was the right thing, but we didn't know
    what to do. I'm sorry for the dishonesty, but I'm not sorry
    for getting her better care.
Therapist: Would you be willing to ask for forgiveness for the
    dishonesty?
Daughter: Yes. That part was wrong.
Therapist: In the old days when a person asked for forgiveness,
    there was usually a visual sign. In some cultures, to show
    a contrite heart or real regret, a person would give a visual
    sign. In some cultures, they would rip their clothes. In some
    cultures, they might shave their heads. Some religious orders
    would wear a sack cloth. But one of the signs of a contrite
    heart in our culture is to ask forgiveness on a bended knee.
    We don't have very many visual signs today. But one of the
    things that I think would help your mother know that you
    are really sorry for the dishonesty is for you to get on a
    bended knee here and let me help you ask forgiveness in a
    special way.
Daughter: (softly) Okay.

The therapist has the daughter kneel to heighten the act. Many
times people ask forgiveness in conversations without taking the

time to apply its specific meaning. However, it is extremely difficult to ask for forgiveness on a bended knee and not reckon with the reality of the hurt. Likewise, it is difficult to have a loved one be humble enough to go on a bended knee and not recognize the significance of the act. As the daughter knelt before the mother and took her hand, the mother protested angrily saying that she might forgive but she would never forget. Probably the mother sensed the powerful position she had in wielding the daughter's dishonesty over her head. If she forgave them, she would lose power. Other issues such as the mother's health would have to be addressed openly if the family overcame this violation. The therapist asked the mother to listen as he coached the daughter.

Therapist: Tell her what you believe you did wrong.

Daughter: I had a part in getting you here under false pretense. I didn't tell you beforehand. I misled you by saying you were coming here to visit me.

Mother: (very nervous) I'm just going to say two or three things here.

Daughter: (taking control) I know. But I want you to hear that I didn't have any intention for you to visit. I always intended to bring you here to the care home.

Mother: (interrupting again) What makes you think that I could be happy here?

Therapist: Now tell her about your feelings.

Daughter: You're my mother and I love you.

Mother: (shifting to a softer tone) I know you do. This whole thing has just hurt.

Therapist: (keeping the daughter on track) Now tell her about your dishonesty in addressing her hurt.

Daughter: Because I misled you and was dishonest to you, I know I have hurt you. I am sorry.

Mother: (sounding genuine and conciliatory) I know you were trying to do the best you could for me. It has just hurt to have been through what I have been through.

Daughter: I need your forgiveness.
Mother: (turning her head away and saying softly and tenderly)
    I forgive you. And for things I did—I know I've done things
    wrong. I did the best I could.

At this point, the mother and daughter spontaneously embraced each other in a powerful moment of mutual forgiveness. The tone and atmosphere of the rest of the session, as well as of succeeding therapy sessions, became lighter; trust returned to the mother/daughter relationship. The mother released the wrong and love and respect replaced much of the anger and distrust. As a result, the mother and the daughters now became free to look at realistic options for the mother, as she continued to decline in physical health.

In later sessions with the daughters, the mother shared some poignant personal memories, especially how she had supported her own mother when she died in her home many years previously. The mother revealed some amusing stories about the early childhood of the adult daughters. This increasing gradient of trust in the family system enabled all four family members to comfort one another and engage in mutual giving.

As the therapy progressed, the mother was no longer angry or depressed. The family struck an agreement that the mother would stay in the personal care home, but that one of the daughters would take the mother back to her previous home one weekend per month. After a year, the three daughters and the mother began the difficult process of discussing the sale of the mother's home. The mutual participation in dealing with the difficult issues of the mother's declining health and her desire for independence was further validation of the increasing justice and trust in the family relationships.

CONCLUSION

Exoneration and forgiveness of family pain and hurt are perhaps the most challenging of interventions with aging families. Issues that have caused the pain often represent long-standing family imbalances. Almost always, the issues have caused severe injustices and distrust. Resulting emotional disturbance and tension in the family is complex. But when successful, exoneration and forgiveness hold tremendous promise for the family. Forgiven hurts, in many cases, strengthen the family to the point where future pains can be handled in a more constructive manner. Exoneration and forgiveness are meaningful and powerful ways to reestablish the balance in the intergenerational family ledger because the acts require the sound relational elements of understanding, love, responsibility, justice, and trust.

In moving an aging family toward exoneration and forgiveness, the therapist must be extremely careful to be partial to each family member's side in the relational reality. It is very seldom that just one member is a destructive "monster" who has wreaked havoc on the rest of the family. Almost always, each person in the relationship has a reason for his or her actions or has been irresponsible in some way. We feel that family pain calls for healing. The contextual framework calls for that healing, not only for the sake of individuals in the current relationships, but also for the sake of the coming generations that will inherit the legacy of the relational imbalances. Healing is difficult and risky work. But the long-range consequences of cutting off from family pain is even riskier and more destructive.

We feel that the four stations of exoneration and forgiveness provide the necessary latitude to work on family pain. We are not suggesting in any way that each hurt that has caused family pain must be addressed directly. Neither are we suggesting that aging family members should open themselves up to untrustworthy actions of others. The four stations of exoneration and forgiveness each takes substantial work and each has a different role in the healing process. In some cases, insight into one's family is a major therapeutic victory. In other cases, the act of forgiveness will be the only thing that will give the members of the relationship relief from their pain. The therapist must always use significant therapeutic judgment in determining how far to go in helping an aging family down this road of exoneration and forgiveness.

9

BALANCING OBLIGATIONS AND ENTITLEMENTS

Things wear out. This is a simple fact of life but not much of a problem in our consumer society. Replacements for that toaster or malfunctioning television are easy to find and in most cases, we afford them without great difficulty. Even some of our favorite things wear out—that dependable refrigerator that we have had for 25 years, that car that has been around since we were married, or that comfortable chair. Although these cherished items are more difficult to replace and throw away, they are still eventually replaced.

All people die. This is also a simple fact of life. However, we have difficulty acknowledging that those people who have had powerful influences on our lives will not be around forever. Like things, people eventually wear out and some will even start to malfunction. Whether it is lack of bladder control or a memory that is deteriorating, most older people find that they do not have the ability to perform as they did when they were younger. But our society has difficulty accepting this fact about people. Somehow we feel that people in order to stay a part of the human race must always function with vigor and be independent and responsible for themselves. Because we have difficulty acknowledging age and death, we also have difficulty knowing what to do with people when they have lost their "usefulness" in terms of offering support, maintaining life-styles, earning wages, or commanding power.

People and things are not the same, but as a society we have a tendency to confuse the two. Things usually have one purpose, but people have multiple purposes and meanings in life and have the unique ability to define new roles and explore new personal vistas during the life course. When things wear out, they are not longer useful. People are different. Each person is an important link with the past and the future. The "usefulness" of people is not found in a role or job, it is found in the contribution—either positive or negative—to this intergenerational linkage. Society has a hard time acknowledging the importance of wisdom and care as a significant contribution to the intergenerational family. Finally, things that are not useful are thrown out or put away. Just because we do not know what to do with older people who can longer contribute in the same way they had in the past is no reason to relegate them to the category of "no longer useful." We must deal with the fact that the aging do shift roles and that they may have different capabilities, but they have a contribution that is vital to the healthy survival of the family.

Some older family members will themselves have this difficulty in distinguishing the usefulness of things and the usefulness of people. These people will feel that to be of any use to their families or society as a whole, they must be independent and make an identifiable daily contribution. But as many older people experience physical or mental deterioration, independence and traditional role contributions start to slip away. It has been our experience that when an older family member realizes the limitations but has difficulty shifting to new roles, the person experiences the relational ledger as being imbalanced. In other words, the older person feels that he or she does not fulfill family obligations and therefore takes from the family more than what is given. Common emotions resulting from these imbalances are guilt from the overbenefitting and fear that relationships will end because they are unfair.

There seem to be three common reactions that older family members have to this fear and guilt. First, many will attempt to hang on to the old roles and independence by becoming rigid in their interactions or beliefs. This will include manipulation of other family members, failure to acknowledge physical or mental limitations, or making up information in an attempt to cover up lack of performance. For instance, a fearful older person may hang on by playing one sibling against the other, may refuse to wear a hearing aid or stop driving a car, or may lie a about being robbed because he or she cannot remember where a purse or wallet was placed.

Second, many older people will lash out at family members and others in an attempt to deal with the emotions of fear and guilt. Many times this lashing out behavior takes the form of projection or paranoia. For instance, an older person may blame his or her failure to eat correctly on the fact that the adult daughter does not buy the right food at the grocery store—even though the older person may no longer be able to open a can or work an oven or microwave. In another example, if the older person is unable to keep track of his or her finances, he or she may accuse a son of trying to steal assets.

A third reaction to the emotion of fear and guilt caused by ledger imbalances is to give up. Older people who take this option do not necessarily deal with the deterioration of aging; they simply give up hope that they will ever be able to perform the old roles. Instead of trying to make significant contributions to the family, these older family members relegate themselves to a position of permanent entitlement. They see themselves as unable to make any contribution and therefore are totally dependent on the family. This giving up behavior may take the form of extreme dependency where the older person does not feel safe or competent to do anything or make any decision without the assistance of another person. In other cases, giving up may mean regression to childlike behaviors. Some older people may use constant physical complaints and ailments to keep family members involved. Any of these reactions drains the family as a whole of emotional energy and trustworthiness in the family deteriorates.

Older people have a definite contribution to make to the intergenerational family. For those who do not have physical or mental limitations, contributions may take the form of work, income, nurturing and education of children, and "kin keeper" through the provision of information to extended family. At minimum, older people at least must fulfill emotional obligations to the family. For instance, older people must talk about the meanings of their lives in the context of the family history in order to help the family make sense out of the past and future. They must talk about the meaning of death and its impact on how one lives life. And older people must protect the family by doing for themselves everything of which they are capable—even walking or eating properly. This protection also extends to acknowledging physical and mental limitations and dealing with the reality those limitations force. But most important, older people must stay connected to the family by functioning in a support role for the younger generations. If the older person insists on being the most important person in the family, the intergenerational unit will stagger as the natural life cycle flow is interrupted.

Finishing well means that the older person adjusts to and moves to meet these new obligations in the intergenerational family ledger. If these obligations are not met, imbalance and unfairness results and trustworthiness deteriorates. We have seen many times very good families that reach the stage of aging and then are unable to adjust and fulfill these obligations. It is sad to witness strong families and fond memories spoiled by the burden of the last several years of unfair relational ledgers. As with any family at any age, fairness and balance are maintained when individuals in the family give to one another. Relational giving earns entitlement. For older people who experience relational imbalances due to not fulfilling obligations, the route to relationships that are fair and trustworthy includes giving to the family and earning entitlement.

As we discussed in Chapter 2, older people and their relationships with their families can be described by a pattern of mutual aid, with older people usually making more of a contribution. It is a smaller percentage of older people, then, that are in this ledger pattern of receiving more than they give. In these cases, ledger imbalances are the root of several kinds of dysfunction and symptomatology (Boszormenyi-Nagy & Ulrich, 1981). The focus of the therapeutic work must be then on helping the aging family achieve a balance in the intergenerational ledger of obligations and entitlement. The following is a case example where balancing these obligations and entitlements becomes essential.

CASE EXAMPLE: EMOTIONAL DISTANCE AND THE "PAIN IN THE CAN"

A 77-year-old widow who was in the early stages of Alzheimer's disease was moved across the country to live in the personal care home that was near her only daughter. The woman also had a son who lived in the state, but the primary caretaking responsibility fell to the daughter. The older woman's health problems stemmed from improper nutrition and hygiene. The daughter had a young adult son and daughter. Although the mother and daughter had an acceptable relationship when they lived in separate states, the daughter's decision to move the mother surfaced many relational difficulties between them. The mother responded with open resentment toward the daughter's efforts to care for her. She would exhibit sudden outbursts of anger and paranoid attitudes and would be extremely belligerent to staff and other residents. She would refuse services such as meals and medication supervision. Both the mother and daughter became increasingly discouraged about their inability to communicate and reason with one another. In the first session with the mother, she revealed to the therapist her concern that she was a burden to her family and that she felt she unfairly benefitted from the relationship with the daughter.

Therapist: Let me ask you this—in looking back over your life,

what would be the thing that you would want to pass along
to your children or grandchildren?

Mother: Humor.

Therapist: Humor?

Mother: Humor. No matter how tough things are, you can always
find something to laugh about. I think that is the best thing
that they could have to carry on down is humor.

Therapist: Well, you do have a very good sense of humor.
(validation)

Mother: You have to. Because you want each day to pass by happy
for us all. There is nothing worse than a pain in the can.
There is nothing worse than someone who is just there to
eat or to sleep or to get this or that. We never have had that
kind of a family.

Therapist: Do you ever think that your children have been a pain
in the can to you?

Mother: Oh no.

Therapist: Have you ever been a pain in the can to them?

Mother: (tentatively) I don't know—because—well, they have
never shown it to me.

Because this family had lived in separate states for many years,
there was limited information on daily or weekly interactions and
relationships. This can be a hindrance to determining imbalances
in the relational ethic dimension. The therapist, therefore, met
with the mother alone for the first eight sessions, using the techniques of life validation and life review. During the first two stages
of therapy, the mother revealed that she came from an immigrant
family and was the eldest of five children. The younger two children died in the Spanish Influenza Epidemic. In her younger
years, the mother was a dancer and traveled with a vaudeville
troop when she was younger. The woman's husband was a musi-
cian and traveled for a time as a director of an orchestra during
the war. After trying their entertainment careers, both husband
and wife settled into working for the state in which they lived.

The woman indeed had a wonderful sense of humor that came out in these initial session. However, tension continued to increase between the mother and daughter, as imbalanced ledger issues continued to be exacerbated by untrustworthy interactions and destructive behavior.

During the life review process, the issues of the woman's past family relationships began to be explored in depth. Distrust, unfairness, and disloyalty—which were current issues between the mother and daughter—were now discussed from an intergenerational perspective. This mother discussed her history with incredible accuracy, given the limitations of her memory. Here she recalls that after she left home at the age of 16 to join the vaudeville team, her parents' marriage slowly drifted apart.

Therapist: As I recall, when you were 16 you left home to join a vaudeville team and things got tough between your parents.

Mother: That's right. We traveled up through Chicago and Canada. We had a lot of work and it was continuous.

Therapist: Tell me about this rift between your parents.

Mother: It was my mother mostly. She wanted to travel with me. I never said that out loud before.

Therapist: Really?

Mother: I was embarrassed by that fact. My mother wanted some of the glory of traveling with me. My father worked as a painter and was a very good painter and he needed someone home to look out for him. Someone to cook for him and do his laundry.

Therapist: So there was a rift because your mother wanted to go with you.

Mother: That's right. She really did want to travel. The main problem was that Father wanted the house to be filled. He wanted to be the head of the house. He worked very hard—he mixed his own paints, moved all the ladders, and he was respected a great deal. He was a gentle man. It caused rifts with my mother because she went to work for the garment

industry. She wanted her own independence from my father.
She wanted her own money. They did piece work in those
days and she was very good so she earned lots of money.
Therapist: So your mother wanted to be independent and your
father wanted her to be at home.
Mother: You know, the funny part of it was that it taught us all
to be independent. In the long run it really did. Eventually,
we all became friends again.

It was obvious to the therapist that this woman had been a part
of the marital struggle between her parents for years. The woman
expressed her loyalty to her father and placed more of the blame
on her mother for the failure of the marriage. When the mother
says out loud that her mother wanted to travel with her for the
first time, there is evidence that the woman had carried this burden with her for years. The evidence would suggest that perhaps
the woman's mother tried to use the daughter's career as an exit
from the marriage. This woman was parentified by her parents
and was probably given much of the responsibility to keep peace
and be the emotional caretaker in the family. The woman alludes
to the emotional pain and imbalance in the family when she tries
to put family independence in a good light by stating that eventually the family became friends again. In the next two sessions,
the woman reveals the pain she felt over being used by her mother
and by the mother's disloyalty to the family after divorcing the
father.

Therapist: So you remember that your father was extremely sad
after he and your mother divorced.
Mother: My father was always a gentle man. It was very seldom
that I heard him raise his temper. But my mother could raise
her temper at the drop of a hat.
Therapist: That is what I understand from your daughter. Your
mother was quite abusive at times.
Mother: (very tentatively) Well, she was very flamboyant. She was

flamboyant in the justifying herself for leaving her husband. Leaving your husband is very, very terrible to a European family. She did these things very flamboyantly to show that she could do very well for herself and that she didn't need anyone.

Therapist: She was successful wasn't she?

Mother: She was. I had to grow old to really understand. Before, I just took everything as a personal bruise for me and my brother and my sister. I was the oldest. I do not remember why I remember these things.

Therapist: They probably hurt.

Mother: They are hurts that I just can't shake. I'm not bruised, but I know why I acted the way I did. I was hurt and I didn't want the other people to know about it.

Therapist: So you covered the hurt.

Mother: I just told them that everyone had their own lives to live and that this one was mine.

The mother is careful in her choice of words because she is hesitant to acknowledge pain and grief. When the therapist uses the word abusive to describe her mother, the woman explains the abuse by describing the behavior as flamboyant. But clearly the woman deals with pain that is still an issue. She covers the pain, but the hurts do not go away. Her declaration to the family about each one living his or her own life is evidence of the emotional distance the family developed as an effort to cover the grief and pain. She describes this process of emotional distance in the family as one of becoming casual friends to each other.

Therapist: Your father was a hard worker and your mother struggled for her own independence.

Mother: That's right. She always had to prove herself. Women, in those days, were not supposed to run a house. They were supposed to leave all decisions to the husband. But my mother would not have it that way.

Therapist: That must have made it difficult not only for your father, but also for you and the other children.

Mother: Well, we were hurt because the people that we loved were separating. We were all getting wise to it—it wasn't going to last too long.

Therapist: You could tell even growing up then that your parents were drifting apart?

Mother: Yes

Therapist: Was that a hurt to you?

Mother: It hurt when my mother and father separated—she went out on a date. That was the hard part and the part that hurt. My father never did go out with another woman. He was always loyal to the family even though mother had abandoned us.

Therapist: So your mother was disloyal to the family?

Mother: She was disloyal to us. We so depended on my mother. We even blamed the death of my two sisters on her. We really tried to blame everything on her.

Therapist: Didn't you move back home when your parents separated?

Mother: Yes. I lived with my mother. As the eldest, I just wanted to be the one to see that the marriage could come back together—which it did not.

Therapist: But you tried.

Mother: But I tried. My mother was really the least dependable. She decided that she deserved some type of happiness because father was demanding. But he was a painter and when he came home he was really tired. He really had to earn his money.

Therapist: So even though your mother was independent, ambitious, and hard working, which was very admirable, she was disloyal to the family. Even with your hard work, you were not able to get them back together.

Mother: No. Once mother made up her mind, she stuck to it. I just don't know anymore about that. Just that my mother and father separated and my mother wanted a divorce and my father would not give her one—of course because she was European and because she was Catholic. All that just tore up everything. We children just felt the pain terribly.

Therapist: I would imagine that it just was awful.

Mother: Being a teenager, I felt in disgrace in my neighborhood.

Therapist: It must have been a very hard time.

Mother: Well, we all tried to put on fronts. It is amazing what tragedy in a family can do to make you grow up faster. The funny thing—we all became—I would say, casual friends after that. We didn't fight as much as we did because we wanted to protect both children and parents.

From the information revealed in the life review, the therapist hypothesized that this mother had fulfilled parental obligations to her family of origin. Parentification usually casts a child into a mediating position between exploitative and manipulative parents (Boszormenyi-Nagy & Krasner, 1986). Although this woman blamed her mother for the marital problems, there is clear evidence that she suffers from split loyalty between her mother and father. She made it apparent in therapy that her mother used her and her career to strike back at her father, but it is safe to assume that the father was also involved in manipulation and exploitation. Trust in this woman's family of origin was understandably depleted. In reaction to this exploitation and imbalance, the woman kept emotional distance from her family. The therapist hypothesized that this woman employed this same emotional distance in her relationship with her husband and children. Most likely, this woman's daughter wanted more of an emotional relationship with her mother when she was growing up. When moderate conflict between mother and daughter developed, emotional distance was maintained.

When the woman's daughter was required to take a more active role in caretaking, the woman became increasingly uncomfortable with the closeness that the relationship required. Caretaking by the daughter required the woman to give up some of her fierce protective distance that she carried over from her family of origin. As hypothesized, the woman's distancing actions of anger and refusal of services were designed to protect her daughter from the pain, grief, and exploitation that this woman experienced with her own mother when she was younger. The woman's fear of over-benefitting from the relationship and of becoming a burden to the daughter was expressed in her thoughts that she would drive her daughter away, just as she had been driven away by the burden of her manipulative mother. Unable to express these relational concerns constructively, the woman resorted to angry and uncooperative behavior.

The aim of this therapeutic intervention was to restimulate trust and balance in the family. The mother needed to gain entitlement in the relationship with her daughter. The therapist ascertained that the first step in the intervention process was to afford the mother the opportunity to give up part of her protective distance. The goal was to involve the daughter in the therapy process and have the mother talk to the daughter about the family, much in the way that she had already talked to the therapist. The mother would give to the daughter by sharing part of her painful past. This would earn the mother entitlement, as the daughter would understand the history and the relational issues of the family more clearly. In the next therapy session, the mother deals with this difficult question of inviting the daughter to therapy.

Therapist: It seems difficult for you to imagine yourself telling your daughter the things you have told me. I'm having trouble understanding.

Mother: Well, for the simple reason. It is my daughter's privilege to talk about herself. Not mine. I have talked to you, but you are not a family friend. You are an outsider who has become a friend. To invite her to come here and talk about things like that—I just can't do that.

Therapist: Okay. Is there some other way that we can let her know about some of the family history without having her here?

Mother: No. She would think that she should have been the first one to hear this history. And she would be right. She is the eldest daughter of this family you and I are always talking about. She would be embarrassed and mad about it all.

The woman first refuses to let the daughter be involved for an interesting reason. In an overt sense, the woman is correct in pointing out that the daughter should have been first to hear the stories. She uses the logic that the trust that has developed between her and the therapist should have been developed first between her and the daughter. This is a reasonable expectation. However, the thought that her daughter would be embarrassed or mad about the past is probably a projection of how this woman had been exploited in the past by her own mother. Therefore, probably in a covert sense, the mother is simply trying to maintain the protective distance. However, the mother recognizes the opportunity to rebuild the trust between her and her daughter as evidenced in her reconsideration to let the daughter be involved later in the same session.

Mother: I would like to talk to her.

Therapist: Well, back to your family history. You have such a wonderful history. Is there some way you can talk . . .

Mother: (interrupting) She would be mad that I told you.

Therapist: She would be mad?

Mother: I think so. I don't know. You see, I have drifted so far away from her. I don't know if I should be the one to attempt to reconcile because I am the older one and should have enough sense to it. I just don't know.

Therapist: But if I got involved in any way, you believe she would be mad.

Mother: Yes—because, after all, you are not family. Not even distantly related family.

Therapist: Except that I care for both of you.

Mother: I know. Is there any way that we could meet?

Therapist: I believe we could arrange it. Your daughter is not that far away. We could probably meet one evening.

Mother: (tentatively) Do you think my daughter would come and follow through?

Therapist: From what I know of your daughter, I think that she would come.

Mother: She would? Let's take a chance at it. After all, she's mine too.

During the first session, the therapist asks the daughter about some of her memories of the family. The mother probably experiences too much discomfort with the closeness required by this session. Perhaps the mother is worried that the daughter will become angry, but more likely that the mother is afraid that the reduction in emotional distance will leave both the mother and daughter vulnerable. The therapist decides here not to press the mother with the hope that the mother will reconsider and expand her effort in the next session.

Daughter: (talking about family vacations) My father would then drive up after we had taken the train and we would all drive back home together.

Mother: (interrupting) Well, come on, daughter. Which way should we go.

Daughter: Does this mean our conversation is over?

Mother: If you want to continue, you are free to. I'm kind of getting sick at my stomach. Like I'm going to throw up. I think a lot of this sentiment is getting down to me.

Therapist: Well then, could we meet again?

Mother: Yes. When she comes back again we will meet.

In the next session, the therapist decided to employ the second step of the intervention process to help the mother initiate care for her daughter and tell her of the family history. The therapist initiated a *need reversal* situation in which the need of the daughter was emphasized over the mother's. The needs of the mother were substantial and obvious, but the corresponding need of the daughter for care, understanding, and appreciation was just as important. This intervention provided the mother with a method of reducing her fear by earning entitlement, while still allowing her to protect her daughter by meeting her needs.

Therapist: I'm wondering if you would be willing to give your daughter what she needs from you or do you believe that your daughter is so independent that she wouldn't take it.

Mother: What does she need from me that she hasn't already gotten?

Therapist: (making an error by hypothesizing about the daughter's needs) I have something in my mind that I would believe she needs from you.

Mother: (as if to challenge the therapist to get back on track) Do you want to talk to her alone about it?

Therapist: (seeking to recover by directing the conversation to the daughter) No. I have something on my mind, but that is my agenda. I don't know if your daughter needs anything from you or not. Why don't we ask her?

Mother: (tenderly turning toward the daughter) I think we are friends as well as mother and daughter—and caring. (turning toward the therapist, with a smile) You will have us both crying.

Therapist: I'm sorry. Of course that is not my intention.

Mother: (laughing) Well it's so touching. (now more seriously) People know that you care for your children very much. And that you have children who can return caring also.

Therapist: (turning to the daughter) What is it that you really need from your mother?

Mother: (interrupting) Tell him you got it all.

Therapist: (encouraging the daughter) Go on.

Daughter: I guess the fact that—uh. (beginning to cry) I brought her here because I care very much for her. I want to be able to keep in touch on a daily basis. I guess what I am beginning to resent is that since mother has been here she has never picked up the phone and called me. Not once in the six months that she has been here.

Mother: Our money isn't going so good, darlin'.

Daughter: It is not long distance. I live across town. All you have to do is pick up the phone and call me.

Demonstrated in this last interchange are the important relational effects that the factual dimension can have on relationships. Although the mother does not call because of relational ledger issues, she probably also has difficulty remembering that she has moved and is only across town from her daughter, instead of being across the country.

Daughter: I come over and spend an evening with you, but you never do reach out for me.

Mother: I'm not aware of that—or at least I wasn't aware of it. I don't want to be a burden to her. That is the biggest word that scares me in my life is burden—burden.

Therapist: I respect that in you because you are such an independent person.

Mother: But you see, it doesn't suit us.

Therapist: This independence doesn't seem to suit both of you. We have identified where you have learned it. I'm just wondering—your daughter is asking you—she needs you to reach out to her. I'm wondering if you can move past the independence to do it.

Mother: I can now because it has all been opened. I do want her caring and I do want to care for her. (turning toward the daughter) I learned today that you were really worried. You thought I was a pain in the can.

Daughter: I never thought you were a pain. I wanted you close so I could care for you and we could care for each other.

Mother: I know that. I am here now. Am I being close enough?

Daughter: (laughing) I like for you to show that you care and appreciate me.

Mother: I do. I always thought that I saw to it that I cared for you. (turning to the therapist) See, you try not to cling too closely to your children and you back away and go to exactly the opposite extreme. I thought I was doing her a favor by releasing her.

Therapist: I think you are wise and correct in what you are saying. You were backing away from your daughter not wanting to be a burden to her but what she really wants is for you to be close. Have you ever heard the phrase, people need to be needed? Maybe your daughter needs to know that you need her.

Daughter: One of things that Mother always said was a goal of parenting was to help your children be as independent as possible as quick as possible. I think that is right and is a worthy goal. (turning the conversation toward the mother) But we all need to know that we are needed and that we are appreciated. I need to know that you appreciate me and that you are glad that I come to see you. Sometimes when I come, you do not even say a word to me.

Mother: Well I thought you were coming out of sheer duty. Honest to God, that was my feeling—not wanting to take you over. (turning toward the therapist) See how—thank you for being here because I'm not sure I could have gotten that out without witness. (tenderly turning back to her daughter) But I thank you. I love you. We will get along much better sweetheart.

Daughter: I know. (as she receives a warm embrace from her mother)

In this session, the daughter was expressing the imbalance she felt in seeking to provide care for her mother and not having the mother respond in an appreciative and caring manner. Although the situation is brought on by the aging process, it is logical to assume that this same imbalance has always existed between the mother and daughter. Yet, the daughter tried to have a more stable and emotionally connected relationship with her mother. Although the mother and daughter at times distance themselves from one another in this session by using conversation with the therapist, the immediate response of the mother is to give to the daughter what she asked for. Her explanation of not wanting to be a burden served as an act of giving. This session provided the mother with the opportunity to give to the daughter; this, in turn, earned the mother entitlement. This earned merit entitled the mother to more of the loving care the daughter was offering.

Since the mother could now directly contribute to the daughter's need with love and affection, the fear and need for protective distance in the relationship abated. A fair balance of give and take was achieved in the family process and a sense of trustworthiness was built. The mother shared more openly about her limitations and frustrations. There were no further outbursts of anger and only an occasional refusal of services. Eventually, with the help of the therapist, the mother fixed a dinner for the daughter's family and shared some of her life history with the grandchildren. Her efforts to expand giving and trustworthiness in the family was further evidence of her lack of need for protective distance.

Therapy in this case lasted 12 sessions. The Alzheimer's disease eventually adversely affected the mother's complete memory and functioning capacity. Even though the daughter now had to face tremendous grief and strain with the mother's deterioration, she still reported that their lives together had produced some of the sweetest times in their entire relationship. The unresolved imbalance was addressed. The daughter and mother connected, despite the disease, and finished the mother's life and their relationship well.

CONCLUSION

Older people often end up in a situation where they may feel that they are a burden to their families. Besides being bad for self-esteem, feeling like a burden often causes feelings of guilt and fear. Older people may think they have little to contribute to the intergenerational group. These imbalances may be handled in the aging family with denial, anger, or depression.

A key element in the process of therapy with an aging family is to realize that all family members are capable of making contributions to the family. For many older people, contributions are made in material ways. But all older people owe to their families the guidance and hope of their wisdom. Although these elements of life are not emphasized in our society as important, it is essential that the therapist tap these resources because these resources are, in fact, essential in order to earn the older person entitlement in the aging family. In addition, these resources are basic to the empowering of intergenerational relationships. The therapeutic intervention of balancing obligations and entitlements means that the therapist initiates the opportunity for the family to earn entitlement with one another and to be able to benefit from the full power of meaning, hope, and wisdom in their lives together.

10

FUTURE TRENDS AND THERAPY WITH AGING FAMILIES

We referred previously to the many dramatic changes that are occurring in the American population. The increase in longevity since 1900 is truly astonishing. Then, 4 percent of the population was over 65; today, the elderly constitute 12 percent of Americans, with greater increase expected. The baby boomers born after World War II will enter the ranks of the elderly by the year 2010. Already, the number of three-, four-and even five-generational families far outnumber what our forefathers experienced.

From a developmental point of view, we are probably ready to conceptualize several new stages in the life cycle: 60 to 80 (the elderly) and those older than 80 (the final stage of life). We have seen that among these elderly cohorts, one must face the critical issues of loss and depression, reduced independence, and chronic illnesses.

FUTURE ISSUES OF AGING AND FAMILY THERAPY

Specialized Training Programs

Across the country in medical schools, there has been an increase in the number of programs that deal with geriatric medicine as an answer to the growing elderly population with specialized medical needs. In a similar fashion, we need programs that train family therapists to offer an emphasis or subspecialty for those therapists who wish to work with aging clients and their families. The coming wave of baby boomers who will become elderly by 2010 will probably create a demand for such family therapists.

Research in Family Therapy with Aging Families

As much of the work with aging families will be in unchartered waters, there is an obvious need for serious research. One important area is that of theoretical frameworks that fit the aging population. This book has attempted to apply contextual family therapy to this specific population. It will be interesting to see applications of other theoretical paradigms, such as structural, strategic, existential and behavioral, to the aging family and its issues.

Another area of research could involve studying the adjustment patterns of widows or widowers in the context of three- or four-generational family systems. More study is needed about new family paradigms that are already developing among the elderly. As people live much longer, we will need to study how elderly sibling relationships fare over many years. Finally, we need to investigate the patterns of relationships among the extended families, both those who live in close proximity and those who are separated by significant geographical distances.

Research is needed in the critical area of ethics, as it affects the care of elderly family members. With recent medical advances, it is quite possible to keep the elderly alive for a long time, even if their capacities are severely reduced. The intergenerational family with ailing, aging members can be faced with questions dealing with the allocation of family resources, the prolongation of life through extraordinary (and often costly) medical care, and equitable sharing of the family's fiscal and emotional resources across three or more generations. Some adult children will face the choice of spending resources, originally destined for their children's education, to keep a grandparent alive. Society faces the question of the allocation of medical resources between care for the very young, especially the poor, and the sustenance of life in the frail, dying elderly.

Mobilization of Family Resources

More and more, family therapists working with aging families will be confronted by the task of facilitating the marshalling of family resources to aid elderly members. One most obvious issue concerns the greater involvement of men in the caretaking role to relieve the overburdened women who are suffering from burn-out as they deal with three or four generations. A second task for family therapists is helping alternative support systems to become involved in the care of the elderly. In this regard, many healthy elderly retired could be enticed away from their televisions to participate in the care of their neighbors and friends. Another challenge to family therapists will be dealing with possible intergenerational tensions that may easily arise from the increasing financial and emotional pressures generated by the care of elderly family members.

New Family Forms

With more couples living together much longer after the departure of their children, one can expect more divorces among the elderly, as well as more second marriages in that same cohort. These new family forms will present the family therapist with special issues, such as step-grandchildren and former step-grandchildren. In this situation, problems arise such as visitation privileges of grandparents or former grandparents, the reactions of adult children to the second marriage of their parents, issues of inheritance, and other emotionally laden relationships.

CONCLUSION

As we near the end of the 20th century, the contrast between the elderly's position in 1900 and the elderly's position in 1992 is marked. The many changes that have occurred over the last 90 years now present family therapists with new challenges as we move toward the 21st century. As a small contribution to meeting these new challenges, we have presented an application of contextual family therapy to work with aging families. It is our hope that this volume will be of help to family therapists who are working with families who have aging members. It is indeed a noble task to help these elderly members deal with unresolved transgenerational family issues before they die. This will then free the younger generations to experience healthier family relationships, as these family members share in the task of the older person—to finish life well.

REFERENCES

Aldous, J. (1987). New views on the family life of the elderly and near elderly. *Journal of Marriage and the Family. 49*, 227–234.

Anderson, W. T. & Hargrave, T. D. (1990). Contextual family therapy and older people: Building trust in the intergenerational family. *Journal of Family Therapy. 12*, 311–320.

Asnes, D. P. (1983). The life validation approach in psychotherapy with elderly patients. *Journal of Geriatric Psychiatry. 16*, 87–97.

Barber, C. (1989). Burden and family care of the elderly and the near elderly. In S. Bahr & E. Peterson (Eds.), *Aging and the Family.* Lexington, Massachusetts: D.C. Health.

Bateson, G. (1972). *Steps to an ecology of the mind.* New York: Ballantine.

Bateson, G., Jackson, D., Haley, J. & Weakland, J. (1956). Toward a theory of schizophrenia. *Behavioral Science. 1*, 251–254.

Bigner, J. J. (1983). *Human development: A lifespan approach.* New York: Macmillian Publishing Company.

Birren, J. E. & Zarit, J. (1985). *Concepts of health, behavior, and aging: Cognition, stress and aging.* Englewood Cliffs: Prentice-Hall.

Black, K. D. & Bengtson, V. L. (1973). Intergenerational relations and continuities in socialization. In P. Baltes & K. W. Schaie (Eds.), *Life-span developmental psychology: Personality and socialization.* New York: Academic Press.

Blau, Z. S. (1981). *Aging in a changing society.* New York: Watts.

Blieszner, R. & Mancini, J. (1987). Enduring ties: Older adults' parental role and responsibilities. *Family Relations. 36*, 176–180.

Boszormenyi-Nagy, I. (1979). Ethical and practical implications of intergenerational family therapy. In J. G. Howells (Ed.), *Advances in family psychiatry* (pp. 446–454). New York: International Universities Press.

Boszormenyi-Nagy, I. (1987). The context of consequences and the limits of therapeutic responsibility. In H. Stierlin, F. B. Simon & G. Schmidt (Eds.), *Familiar realities: The Heidelberg conference* (pp. 41–51). New York: Brunner/Mazel.

Boszormenyi-Nagy, I. & Krasner, B. (1980). Trust-based therapy: A contextual approach. *American Journal of Psychiatry. 137*, 767–775.

Boszormenyi-Nagy, I. & Krasner, B. (1986). *Between give and take: A clinical guide to contextual therapy*. New York: Brunner/Mazel.

Boszormenyi-Nagy, I. & Spark, G. (1984). *Invisible loyalties*. New York: Brunner/Mazel.

Boszormenyi-Nagy, I. & Ulrich, D. N. (1981). Contextual family therapy. In A. S. Gurman & D. P. Kniskern (Eds.), *Handbook of family therapy* (pp. 159–186). New York: Brunner/Mazel.

Bowen, M. (1978). *Family therapy in clinical practice*. New York: Jason Aronson.

Brody, E. (1985). Parent care as a normative family stress. *The Gerontologist. 25*, 19–29.

Brody, E. M. (1990). Role reversal: An inaccurate and destructive concept. *Journal of Gerontological Social Work. 15*, 15–22.

Brubaker, T. H. (1985). *Later life families*. Beverly Hills, California: Sage Publications.

Buber, M. (1958). *I and thou*. New York: Charles Scribner's Sons.

Butler, R. N. (1963). The life review: An interpretation of reminiscence in the aged. *Psychiatry. 26*, 65–76.

Butler, R. N. (1975). *Why survive? Being old in America*. New York: Harper & Row.

Butler, R. N. (1985). Health, productivity, and aging: An overview. In R. N. Butler & H. P. Gleason (Eds.), *Productive aging: Enhancing vitality in later life* (pp. 1–13). New York: Springer Publishing Company.

Butler, R. N. & Lewis, M. I. (1983). *Aging and mental health: Positive psychological approaches*. St. Louis: C. V. Mosby.

Butler, R. N. & Lewis, M. I. (1991). *Aging and mental health*. New York: Merrill.

Carter, B. & McGoldrick, M. (1988). Overview: The changing family life cycle—A framework for family therapy. In B. Carter & M.

McGoldrick (Eds.), *The changing family life cycle (2nd ed.)* (pp. 3–28). New York: Gardner Press.

Chambers, C. D., White, O. Z., Lindquist, J. H. & Harter, M. T. (1987). Medical mood alteration among the elderly: Victimization or deviancy? In C. D. Chambers, J. H. Lindquist, O. Z. White, & M. T. Harter (Eds.), *The elderly: Victims and deviants* (pp. 56–71). Athens, Ohio: Ohio University Press.

Cicirelli, V. G. (1981). *Helping elderly parents: The role of adult children*. Boston, Massachusetts: Auburn House Publishing.

deVries, H. A. (1983). Physiology of exercise and aging. In D. S. Woodruff & J. E. Birren (Eds.), *Aging: Scientific perspectives and social issues (2nd ed.)*. Monterey, California: Brooks/Cole Publishing Company.

Dobson, J. E. & Dobson, R. L. (1985). The sandwich generation: Dealing with aging parents. *Journal of Counseling and Development. 63*, 572–574.

Dowd, J. & LaRossa, R. (1982). Primary group contact and elderly morale: An exchange/power analysis. *Sociology and Social Research. 66*, 184–197.

Duvall, E. M. & Hill, R. L. (1948). *Report to the committee on the dynamics of family interaction*. Washington, D.C.: National Conference on Family Life.

Erikson, E. H. (1963). *Childhood and society (2nd ed.)*. New York: Norton & Company.

Erikson, E. H. (1985). *The life cycle completed: A review*. New York: Norton & Company.

Erikson, E. H., Erikson, J. M. & Kivnick, H. Q. (1986). *Vital involvement in old age*. New York: Norton & Company.

Fairbairn, W. R. (1963). Synopsis of an object relations theory of the personality. *International Journal of Psychoanalysis. 44*, 224.

Framo, J. L. (1976). Family of origin as a therapeutic resource for adults in marital and family therapy: You can and should go home again. *Family Process. 15*, 193–210.

Framo, J. L. (1981). The integration of marital therapy with sessions with family of origin. In A. S. Gurman & D. P. Kniskern (Eds.), *Handbook of family therapy* (pp. 133–158). New York: Brunner/Mazel.

France, A. I. (1990). Psychology of aging: Stability and change in intelligence and personality. In K. F. Ferraro (Ed.), *Gerontology: Perspectives and issues* (pp. 58–86). New York: Springer Publishing Company.

Gurman, A. S. & Kniskern, D. P. (1981). Editor's note. In A. S. Gurman & D. P. Kniskern (Eds.), *Handbook of family therapy* (p. 185). New York: Brunner/Mazel.

Haley, J. (1987). *Problem solving therapy, (2nd ed.)*. San Francisco: Jossey-Bass.

Hargrave, T. D., Jennings, G. & Anderson, W. T. (1991). The development of a relational ethics scale. *Journal of Marital and Family Therapy. 17*, 145–159.

Havighurst, R. J. (1972). *Human development (2nd ed.)*. New York: David McKay Company.

Hess, B. & Waring, J. M. (1978). Changing patterns of aging and family bonds in later life. *Family Coordinator. 27*, 303–314.

Horne, J. (1985). Caregiving: Helping an aging loved one. Glenview, Illinois: Scott and Foresman.

Johnson, C. L. (1985). Grandparenting options in divorcing families: An anthropological perspective. In V. L. Bengtson & J. F. Robertson (Eds.), *Grandparenthood*. Beverly Hills, California: Sage Publications.

Johnson, E. S. & Bursk, B. J. (1977). Relationships between the elderly and their adult children. *The Gerontologist. 17*, 90–96.

Johnson, R. P. (1988). How to stay young in a fast aging world: Part II. *Co-Op Networker: Caregivers of Older Persons. 4*, 1–4.

Kaslow, F. W. (1987). Marital and family therapy. In M. B. Sussman & S. K. Steinmetz (Eds.), *Handbook of marriage and the family* (pp. 835–859). New York: Plenum Press.

Kastenbaum, R. (1977). *Death, society, and human experience*. St. Louis: C. V. Mosby.

Kuhn, M. (1987). Politics and aging: The gray panthers. In L. L. Carstensen & B. A. Edelstein (Eds.), *Handbook of clinical gerontology* (pp. 376–386). New York: Pergamon Press.

Lee, G. R. (1979). Children and the elderly: Interaction and morale. The case of the United States. *Aging and Society. 5*, 19–38.

Lee, G. & Ellithorpe, E. (1982). Intergenerational exchange and subjective well being among the elderly. *Journal of Marriage and the Family.* *44*, 217–224.

Long, J. K. & Mancini, J. A. (1990). Aging couples and the family system. In T. H. Brubaker (Ed.), *Family relationships in later life (2nd ed.)* (pp. 29–48). Newbury Park, California: Sage Publications.

Longino, C. F., Soldo, B. J., & Manton, K. G. (1990). Demography of aging in the United States. In K. F. Ferraro (Ed.), *Gerontology: Perspectives and issues* (pp. 19–41). New York: Springer Publishing Company.

Madanes, C. (1984). *Behind the one-way mirror.* San Francisco: Jossey-Bass.

Mancini, J. (1979). Family relationsips and morale among people 65 years of age and older. *American journal of orthopsychiatry.* *49*, 292–300.

Mancini, J. & Blieszner, R. (1986). Successful aging and close relationships with children. Paper presented at the 39th meeting of the Gerontological Society of America, Chicago, Illinois.

Mancini, J. & Blieszner, R. (1989). Aging parents and adult children. *Journal of marriage and the family.*

Maslow, A. H. (1970). *Motivation and personality (2nd ed.).* New York: Harper & Row.

McGoldrick, M. & Gerson, R. (1985). *Genograms in family assessment.* New York: Norton & Company.

Minuchin, S. (1974). *Families and family therapy.* Cambridge: Harvard University Press.

Minuchin, S. & Fishman, H. C. (1981). *Family therapy techniques.* Cambridge: Harvard University Press.

Mischel, W. (1981). *Introduction to personality (3rd ed.).* New York: Holt, Rinehart & Winston.

Morgan, L. (1984). Changes in family interaction following widowhood. *Journal of Marriage and the Family.* *46*, 323–331.

Moss, M., Moss, S. Z. & Moles, E. L. (1985). The quality of relationships between elderly parents and their out-of- town children. *The Gerontologist.* *25*, 134–140.

Myers, J. E. (1988). The mid/late life generation gap: Adult children with aging parents. *Journal of Counseling and Development.* *66*, 331–335.

Myers, J. E. (1989). *Adult children and aging parents.* Dubuque, Iowa: Kendall/Hunt Publishing Company.

National Center for Health Statistics. (1988). *Health, United States, 1987*. Washington, D.C.: United States Government Printing Office.

Neugarten, B. L., Havighurst, R. J. & Tobin, S. S. (1968). Personality and patterns of aging. In B. L. Neugarten (Ed.), *Middle age and aging* (pp. 173–177). Chicago: The University of Chicago Press.

Newman, B. M. & Newman, P. R. (1983). *Understanding adulthood*. New York: Holt, Rinehart & Winston Publishing Company.

Newman, B. M. & Newman, P. R. (1991). *Development through life: A psychosocial approach (5th ed)*. Pacific Grove, California: Brooks/Cole Publishing Company.

Peck, R. C. (1968). Psychological development in the second half of life. In B. L. Neugarten (Ed.), *Middle age and aging*. Chicago: The University of Chicago Press.

Petersen, D. M. (1987). Drug use and misuse in old age. In C. D. Chambers, J. H. Lindquist, O. Z. White, & M. T. Harter (Eds.), *The elderly: Victims and deviants* (pp. 24–55). Athens, Ohio: Ohio University Press.

Quinn, W. H. (1983). Personal and family adjustment in later life. *Journal of Marriage and the Family. 45*, 57–73.

Raffoul, P. R., Cooper, J. K. & Love, D. W. (1981). Drug misuse in older people. *The Gerontologist. 21*, 146–150.

Reichard, S., Livson, F. & Peterson, P. G. (1962). *Aging and personality: A study of 87 older men*. New York: Wiley Publishing Company.

Riley, M. W. & Foner, A. (1968). *Aging and society, Volume I: An inventory of research findings*. New York: Russell Sage.

Rockstein, M. J. & Sussman, M. (1979). *Biology of aging*. Belmont, California: Wadsworth.

Schefft, B. K. & Lehr, B. K. (1990). Psychological problems of older adults. In K. F. Ferraro (Ed.), *Gerontology: Perspectives and issues* (pp. 283–293). New York: Springer Publishing Company.

Seltzer, M. M. (1990). Role reversal: You don't go home again. *Journal of Gerontological Social Work. 15*, 5–14.

Shanas, E. (1979). The family as a social support system in old age. *The Gerontologist. 19*, 169–174.

Shanas, E. (1980). Older people and their families: The new pioneers. *Journal of Marriage and the Family. 42*, 9–15.

Sheehan, N. W. & Nuttall, P. (1988). Conflict, emotion, and personal strain among family caregivers. *Family Relations. 37*, 92–98.

Smedes, L. B. (1984). *Forgive and forget.* New York: Harper & Row.

Smith, G. C., Smith, M. F. & Toseland, R. W. (1991). Problems identified by family caregivers in counseling. *The Gerontologist. 31*, 15–22.

Smith, S. L. (1991). *Making peace with your family.* New York: Plenum Press.

Special Committee on Aging. (1983). *Developments in aging: 1983, Volume 1.* Washington, D.C.: United States Government Printing Office.

Stierlin, H. (1973). A family perspective on adolescent runaways. *Archives of General Psychiatry. 12*, 56–62.

Thomae, H. (1985). Psychology of aging: Personality and its attributes. In J. C. Brocklehurst (Ed.), *Textbook of geriatric medicine and gerontology* (pp. 105–121). Edinburgh: Churchill Livingston.

Thompson, L. (1989). Contextual and relational morality: Intergenerational responsibility in later life. In J. Mancini (Ed.), *Aging parents and adult children.* Lexington: D.C. Health.

Timberlake, E. M. (1980). The value of grandchildren to grandmothers. *Journal of Gerontological Social Work. 3*, 63–76.

Treas, J. (1983). Aging and the family. In D. S. Woodruff & J. E. Birren (Eds.), *Aging: Scientific perspectives and social issues* (pp. 92–108). Los Angeles: University of California.

Treas, J. & Bengtson, V. L. (1987). The family in later years. In M. B. Sussman & S. K. Steinmetz (Eds.), *Handbook of marriage and the family* (pp. 625–648). New York: Plenum Press.

Troll, L. E. (1982). *Continuations: Adult development and aging.* Monterey, California: Brooks/Cole.

Troll, L., Miller, S. & Atchley, R. (1979). *Families in later life.* Belmont, California: Wadsworth.

Ulrich, D. N. (1983). Contextual family and marital therapy. In B. Wolman & G. Stricker (Eds.), *Handbook of family and marital therapy* (pp. 187–211). New York: Plenum Press.

United States Bureau of the Census. (1987a). *American centenarians: Data from the 1980 Census, Series P-23, Number 153.* Washington, D.C.: United States Government Printing Office.

United States Bureau of the Census. (1987b). *Estimates of the population of the United States, by age, sex, and race, 1980 to 1986, Series P-25, Number 1000.* Washington, D.C.: United States Government Printing Office.

Van Heusden, A. & Van Den Eerenbeemt, E. (1987). *Balance in motion.* New York: Brunner/Mazel.

Walsh, F. (1988). The family in later life. In B. Carter & M. McGoldrick (Eds.), *The changing family life cycle (2nd ed.)* (pp. 311–332). New York: Gardner Press.

Whitaker, C. (1982). *From psyche to system, the evolving theory of Carl Whitaker.* J. Neil & D. Kniskern (Eds.). New York: Guilford Press.

Williamson, D. (1981). Personal authority via termination of the intergenerational hierarchical boundary: A new stage in the family life cycle. *Journal of Marital and Family Therapy. 7,* 441–452.

Willott, J. F. (1990). Neurongerontology: The aging nervous system. In K. F. Ferraro (Ed.), *Gerontology: Perspectives and issues* (pp. 58–86). New York: Springer Publishing Company.

Wolfe, S. M., Fugate, L., Hulstrand, E. P. & Kamimoto, L. E. (1988). *Worst pills, best pills: The older adult's guide to avoiding drug-induced death or illness.* Washington, D.C.: Public Citizen Health Research Group.

Wolinsky, M. A. (1990). *A heart of wisdom: Marital counseling with older and elderly couples.* New York: Brunner/Mazel.

Zarit, J. M. & Zarit, S. H. (1987). Molar aging: Physiology and psychology of normal aging. In L. L. Carstensen & B. A. Edelstein (Eds.), *Handbook of clinical gerontology* (pp. 376–386). New York: Pergamon Press.

Zarit, S. & Zarit, J. (1982). Families under stress: Interventions for caregivers of senile dementia patients. *Psychotherapy. 19,* 461–471.

Zopf, P. E. (1986). *America's older population.* Houston, Texas: Cap and Gown Press.

NAME INDEX

Aldous, J., 19
Anderson, W. T., xi, 5–6, 54, 59, 88–89
Asnes, D. P., xii, 70, 92, 100–101
Atchley, R., 21

Barber, C., 17, 19
Bateson, G., 84
Bengston, V. L., 14, 19
Bigner, J. J., 31, 32
Birren, J. E., 30
Black, K. D., 19
Blau, Z. S., 21
Blieszner, R., 17, 19, 21
Bonjean, M., xiii
Boszormenyi-Nagy, I., xiii–xiv, 45–46, 47, 48, 51, 54, 57, 58, 59, 62, 82, 86, 88, 126, 128, 129, 132, 150–151, 171, 177
Bowen, M., 7, 45
Brody, E., 13, 17–18
Brubaker, T. H., 17
Buber, M., 54
Bursk, B. J., 19
Butler, R. N., xii, 4, 10, 11, 14, 22, 28, 37, 60, 71, 78, 92, 109, 110–111, 112–113, 114

Carter, B., 4–5, 6, 8
Chambers, C. D., 81
Cicirelli, V. G., 21, 23
Cooper, J. K., 81

de Vries, H. A., 32
Dobson, J. E., 9
Dobson, R. L., 9

Dowd, J., 21
Duvall, E. M., 6

Ellithorpe, E., 21–22
Erikson, E. H., 11, 14, 15, 16, 35, 36, 37, 48–51, 82, 92, 110
Erikson, J. M., 11, 14, 15, 16, 82

Fairbairn, W. R., 48
Fishman, H. C., 53, 111
Foner, A., 22
Framo, J. L., 45
France, A. I., 38
Freud, S., 35
Fugate, L., 81

Gerson, R., 81
Gurman, A. S., 46

Haley, J., 53, 84
Hargrave, T. D., xiv, 5–6, 54, 59, 88–89
Harter, M. T., 81
Havighurst, R. J., 37, 38
Hess, B., 19
Hill, R. L., 6
Horne, J., 19
Hulstrand, E. P., 81

Jackson, D., 84
Jennings, G., ix, 54, 88–89
Johnson, C. L., 16
Johnson, E. S., 19
Johnson, R. P., 18

199

SUBJECT INDEX